Holiday Readers Theatre

Similar Titles of Interest from Teacher Ideas Press

Frantic Frogs and Other Frankly Fractured Folktales for Readers Theatre by Anthony D. Fredericks

Readers Theatre for Beginning Readers by Suzanne I. Barchers

Readers Theatre for Children: Scripts and Script Development by Mildred Knight Laughlin and Kathy Howard Latrobe

Readers Theatre for Young Adults: Scripts and Script Development by Kathy Howard Latrobe and Mildred Knight Laughlin

Social Studies Readers Theatre for Children: Scripts and Script Development by Mildred Knight Laughlin, Peggy Tubbs Black, and Margery Kirby Loberg

Social Studies Readers Theatre for Young Adults: Scripts and Script Development by Kathy Howard Latrobe, Carol Casey, and Linda A. Gann

Holiday Readers Theatre

Charla R. Pfeffinger

Teacher Ideas Press
A Division of
Libraries Unlimited, Inc.
Englewood, Colorado
1994

This book is dedicated to my children,
Christine and Joseph.

Printed in the United States of America

TEACHER IDEAS PRESS
A Division of
Libraries Unlimited, Inc.
P.O. Box 6633
Englewood, CO 80155-6633
1-800-237-6124

Stephen Haenel, Project Editor
Deborah Korte, Copy Editor
Ann Marie Damian, Proofreader
Kay Minnis, Design and Layout

Library of Congress Cataloging-in-Publication Data

Pfeffinger, Charla R.
Holiday readers theatre / Charla R. Pfeffinger.
ix, 181 p. 22x28 cm.
Includes bibliographical references.
ISBN 1-56308-162-8
1. Holidays--Exercises, recitations, etc. 2. Children's plays, American. 3. Holidays--Juvenile drama. I. Title.
PS3566.F39H65 1994
812'.54--dc20 94-3823
CIP

Contents

Acknowledgments

I would like to thank the 1992-93 seventh-graders of Rankin School, Pekin, Illinois, who not only read the scripts for me, which helped with the flow of the dialogue, but also served as inspiration for the characters in "Fright Night." I also want to thank Mrs. Gilbert and her third-graders, who listened so intently to each of our scripts as we performed them.

Introduction

THE ROLE OF READERS THEATRE

In the presentation of a readers theatre script, a narrator and two or more readers interpret a literary work. The interpretation enables the audience to fully understand the content of the script through the use of characterization, settings, and movement by the readers. Because movement is optional, there is little need to practice blocking and timing. Vocal interpretation of the material should be the focal point both of the few necessary run-throughs and of the presentation itself.

Readers theatre scripts are read, not memorized. This alleviates some of the fear students have of participating in a presentation. However, it does put the emphasis on effective reading skills. Props can be a wonderful addition to any script, but they should be kept to a minimum so they do not overshadow the reading. Readers theatre can be easily incorporated into the whole language program and works nicely with the Discorse System™, the current trend among middle schools. These scripts offer the teacher an exciting way to enhance existing programs during the holiday seasons as they are celebrated in the school system. The scripts lend themselves to use with theme teaching, an eclectic approach to teaching a subject, as well as use in content areas in the classroom.

The scripts in this book relate to some of the holidays celebrated during the school year and are arranged chronologically. Some of these scripts are adaptations of various authors' works, whereas others are original pieces based on my research on the particular holiday. Many of the adapted pieces have had the language and dialects modernized for the ease of the younger reader. Through this process the reader may more readily paraphrase the script, keeping it in the reader's own language pattern. This is a completely acceptable practice and should be encouraged if the reader is having problems with a passage, as long as the meaning of the passage is not lost as the student paraphrases.

PREPARING THE SCRIPTS

Once a script has been chosen for the class to read, make enough copies so that the teacher, the narrator, and each character has one. Make an extra copy in case a script is lost. Encourage students to underline or highlight their parts in the script.

Scripts can be stored in a number of ways. Folders or binders with brads provide both easy storage and easy page turning. File folders can also be used. In this case, pages should be stapled in securely or yarn used to secure the scripts through punched holes; brads, in this type of a system, tend to pull loose easily. The title of the script should be printed on each folder, allowing for easy storage for later use. The student's name can also be applied with a file label, which can be recovered with the name of a new reader the following year. An older student or parent can be assigned to prepare the folders and scripts if your students are too young to have mastered this skill.

GETTING STARTED

Readers theatre scripts come with a varying number of readers. On holidays where a number of alternatives are offered, you may want to prepare more than one script to involve a larger number of student readers. If you are introducing holiday readers theatre scripts in the fall and plan to begin with Labor Day, you may want to pair two people to read the same part, as there is only one Labor Day script and it has a limited number of roles. Readers theatre is an exercise in reading, not memorizing, and pairing readers allows more students to be involved in script reading. If you present this script to another class or to the members of your own class, however, select only one reader to actually present the part. Remind those students who were not selected that there are many holidays ahead and everyone will have the chance to present a role during the school year.

In introducing the scripts to the group as a whole, the teacher should point out that the scripts are meant to be read, not memorized. She or he should also point out that the first few sections of each script provide information for the teacher; they are not reading lines for the students. All of these scripts begin with the narrator, so students may want to star the narrator's first lines so they do not get lost as they practice when you are not with them. When the first script is introduced to the class, students should all read through the parts out loud. The younger children will all want a part, so it is imperative that the teacher make wise use of readers and find important supporting roles for the other children.

Whether you assign the parts or have try-outs for each reading part, keep in mind the difficulty of the vocabulary for each of the parts, as well as any reading habits particular students may have that might make them difficult to listen to as oral readers. Less skilled readers can be used as understudies or practice partners as the students work on their scripts. Not only will this make them feel useful, but it will help them improve their reading skills in a more informal setting. This enables the reluctant readers to learn new vocabulary and stretch their reading potential as they become more familiar with the scripts. It also ensures that you have a full complement of readers when you get ready to present your script. Because our class prepared scripts for other classes in lower grades, it was difficult to reschedule presentations if readers were absent. It is equally difficult to substitute a reader who has never seen the script or participated in the group practices. Practice readers can save the performance, even if their ability may not be at the level of the missing reader. Middle school students who are looking for their niche will often want the more important or involved roles. If you are unable to accommodate them, it is extremely important that they perceive their assigned roles, whatever they may be, to be more important than the ones they originally wanted. Working as understudies, particularly for major roles, gives less skilled readers a smaller role in the actual performance, but it also makes them feel important.

The goal of readers theatre is to develop and inspire competent readers outside of the usual curriculum. It also allows them to enjoy literature they might not otherwise read on their own. Although teachers often want students to read only those scripts at grade level, for the reluctant readers, reading a script designed for younger readers, even if it seems a bit childish to you, may become quite an impressive presentation once these readers have worked together, because they will want to compete against the more accomplished readers. Reluctant readers are also good choices for the parts of younger children. Their halting reading style often is representative of how some smaller children speak to adults.

Those students who are reluctant to read or who are not readers in the current presentation can preview other scripts for later use, prepare props, or make advertisement flyers for the presentation. There may be a nonreader or two who can visualize staging and would make a good director or prompter if you find these positions are necessary.

PRESENTATION SUGGESTIONS

The physical arrangement of readers generally follows the same format in each script. Students sit on stools or chairs while the narrator stands at a lectern or a music stand off to one side of the presentation area. However, you will find that this suggestion is just that, a suggestion. Some scripts in this book suggest different arrangements of the stools or chairs to indicate different scenes in the script. Also, I have found that many students prefer to move, as they are not good at sitting still. This may be another consideration in casting a script. If you have several students who find sitting difficult, do not assign them to a group of students who prefer to sit while they present the script. Whether they sit, stand, or move as they present their script is dependent on what makes them most comfortable. Any suggestions given at the beginning of the script can be used as a starting point for the readers, letting them expand from that suggestion as they feel comfortable.

Many of these scripts do lend themselves to movement. Students must feel comfortable with movement on the staging area, as well as entering and exiting the stage. They need to be reminded that their audience is in front of them and they must not turn their backs to the viewers. It is good to have a nonreader work with these students as they practice to remind them where the audience is and to make suggestions if their movement is too busy. Those readers who like to leave the performance area as they are delivering their final lines must be instructed to exit *after* they have finished talking. Some students will want to stay onstage long after their reading is done and try to steal the scene. Peer pressure will quickly cure this problem.

Because many of these holiday readers theatre scripts are based on historical events, they tend to feature male roles. Where this is the case, female students may be assigned the part of the narrator. Where the narration is longer, it can be divided among several girls. Of course, females can also be assigned to read male parts; readers do not have to match the designated sex of the role. When appropriate, the teacher may want to photocopy the script and change the role name(s) using correction fluid before copies are made for the readers.

PROPS

Traditionally props are not a part of readers theatre scripts. However, in many of the scripts in this book, props are often suggested. These are not necessary, but they do enhance the presentation. Prop making can be a class art project or the responsibility of the nonreaders. In "The Secret of the Mardi Gras," for example, masks for the readers, and the class as a whole, would enhance this story, as would the movement of the parade. In other stories, students and teachers can identify those things they want for props or costumes. Emphasis should remain on the reading at all times; if props become cumbersome or distracting, they should be eliminated.

DELIVERY

It is important that students learn to use their voices as the means of expressing their characters' feelings and ideas. To achieve good voice control and recognize changes in vocal expression that indicate responses to different events, students should take part in a variety of voice exercises. In these warm-ups, the entire class responds to a prompt that will help them understand expression. Following are some suggestions:

- discovering school has been canceled due to snow
- being grounded because of poor grades
- learning your best friend is moving
- learning your best friend has lied to you
- learning you are going on a dream trip
- being told you won't have a test on Monday
- being told your parents are going to visit your class all day

Once expression has been examined and students are aware of the need to change their vocal tones while reading, the next challenge is learning how to read a script properly. It is imperative that the students hold their scripts at a proper angle so they do not have their heads buried in the script or their faces covered by the script. Though they do not have to memorize the script, they do need to focus on a point offstage, which will help them keep their heads up so their voices can be heard. Students can learn to look in the audience's eyes, at a point on the back wall, like a clock, or at one person in the back of the room. Onstage the focal point should be the person they are talking with. Notice I say "with" and not "to." They do need to understand that this is dialogue, which calls for responses, not just sentences that are being said.

If you are interested in using simple action, such as pretending to be asleep, eating, and so forth, mime is an excellent way to teach these skills. Students can practice mime by performing simple tasks at their desks, such as brushing their hair, eating, making a phone call, writing a letter, or putting on happy or sad expressions. After this exercise, select some actions in the script you are using and have the class as a whole practice these in mime at their desks. The action does not have to be big or exaggerated. The more simple the action, the more effective. Once students have become familiar with mime, it can be incorporated into a script. When using mime, students must remember to face the audience so that facial expressions and movements can be seen.

THE AUDIENCE

Although we do not often consider the audience as having a role in readers theatre, for the very young or new readers to this format, it is important to teach them how to respond to the performance. They need to learn when it is appropriate to laugh and how to laugh. They need to understand the use of applause at the end of the script or at scene changes. They also need to be instructed on when to be viewers only and when it is okay to express a reaction. Cue cards can be used, with rebuses or words, to indicate an appropriate audience reaction. For instance, using a card that says "APPLAUSE" or shows two hands clapping may be a good way to teach viewers when to applaud. A happy face may indicate laughter, whereas a finger held up to the lips could indicate quiet so that laughter does not continue over the next reader's lines.

It is also necessary to teach the readers how to respond to an audience. They need to know how long to wait for the audience's laughter to stop, how to ignore unnecessary outbursts from students, and how to react to one another when the readers become confused or giggly as a response to the audience. It is easy for a very young audience to cause confusion among readers with their unexpected responses. The readers need to be prepared to react and know how to assert themselves over their audience to continue the reading.

BEYOND READERS THEATRE FOR READERS

Being a reader will not be enough for some students and many teachers. Becoming writers of class scripts is the next logical step and should fit nicely into your language arts program, whether you encourage students to write their own individual scripts or you work on a script together as a class. Reluctant readers may flourish as writers, finding a new way to express themselves. The easiest way to begin is to find a simple story with dialogue and put it into a script form. This teaches the students how to extract conversation from a story. The nondialogue text can then be condensed and converted into narration. For a more in-depth study of this process, consult part 1 of Shirlee Sloyer's 1982 book, *Readers Theatre: Story Dramatization in the Classroom.*

SOURCES

Barchers, Suzanne I. *Readers Theatre for Beginning Readers.* Englewood, CO: Teacher Ideas Press, 1993.

Bauer, Caroline Feller. *Read for the Fun of It: Active Programming with Books for Children.* Ill. by Lynn Gates Bredeson. Bronx, NY: H. W. Wilson, 1992.

Laughlin, Mildred Knight, and Kathy Howard Latrobe. *Readers Theatre for Children: Scripts and Script Development.* Englewood, CO: Teacher Ideas Press, 1990.

Sloyer, Shirlee. *Readers Theatre: Story Dramatization in the Classroom.* Urbana, IL: National Council of Teachers of English, 1982.

New Year's Eve

A New Year's Talk*

BACKGROUND INFORMATION

It is the eve of a New Year. Traditionally, the Old Year is portrayed as an old man and the New Year as a baby. With this in mind, the author has put together a humorous conversation between the outgoing Old Year and the incoming New Year. The New Year is obviously concerned about making the year flow smoothly, and the Old Year, mature and wise, is well aware that it is fruitless to tell the young what to do; they must experience things for themselves. However, before departing, completing another rite of passage, the Old Year leaves the New Year with a few things to consider as he takes over.

STAGING

The Narrator can stand or sit to the right of the performance area. Old Year should be sitting stage center while the Narrator reads the introduction. New Year should enter at the end of the narration.

CHARACTERS

Narrator, New Year, and Old Year.

*Adapted from Lauren Richards, "A New Year's Talk," in *Merry Christmas to You* (New York: E. P. Dutton, 1965).

A New Year's Talk

Narrator:

It is New Year's Eve. It is tradition that a baby represents the new year, and a very old man represents the old year. This story is about the meeting of the old and new years as midnight nears on December 31st. It is time for the old year to give advice to the new year and then to leave and let the new year take over.

New Year:

Here I am.

Old Year:

Oh! Here you are, eh? Come in and let me have a look at you. Shut the door after you, please.

New Year:

Frosty night. It is fine and clear, though. I have had a delightful journey.

Old Year:

Humph! I don't expect to find it delightful as I leave. In this cold, the rain racks my bones. A long, cold drive, I'd say. To be sure, I thought it was pleasant when I was your age, youngster. Is the sleigh waiting?

New Year:

Yes, but there is no hurry. Wait a bit and tell me about this place.

Old Year:

Things could have been better. Yet, I guess they might have been worse, too. They were worse before I came, much worse. I have done a great deal to make things better. Now I expect you to follow my example. If you do, it will be a good year.

New Year:

I shall do my best. Depend upon it! Now tell me a little about what I must do.

Old Year:

In the first place, you have the weather to attend to. You have a clerk to help you with that, but he is not always reliable. There is a great deal of work to be done in the weather department. The seasons have a way of running into each other. Then they get mixed up, if you don't keep a sharp eye on them. The months are a troublesome, unruly set. You must also be careful how you hand out wet and dry weather. Your reputation depends a great deal on that. And one thing I want you to do very carefully. Watch the leaves that are turned.

New Year:

I thought Autumn took care of that.

Old Year:

I don't mean the leaves on the trees. You see, at the beginning of every year, half of the people in the world say, "I am going to turn over a new leaf." That means they intend to behave themselves better in the new year. As a rule, these leaves do not stay turned over for long. I know a great many little boys who promised me to turn over a new leaf in regard to tearing their clothes, losing things, and bringing mud into the house. And little girls who promised they were going to keep their dresser drawers tidy and their clothes neat. But I didn't see much of that after a few days of the new year had gone by. They all seemed to go back to their old ways.

New Year:

I'll attend to it. Any other suggestions?

Old Year:

Well, I have never found that young people, or young years, were good at taking advice. You must go your own way. Don't come up with any new inventions. There have been quite enough lately. Above all, you must take care of the children. And remember—good weather. Now the horses are getting impatient. My time is nearly up, so I shall start on my long drive. You will find everything in pretty good shape, even though you may think of me as an old fogey. Perhaps I am. Good-bye, New Year. Good luck to you.

A Child's March to a Dream

BACKGROUND INFORMATION

Martin Luther King, Jr., was born in Atlanta, Georgia, on January 15, 1929. His father was the Reverend Martin Luther King, known as Daddy King. His mother was Alberta Williams, known as Mother Dear. Martin, whose nickname was M.L., had an older sister, Christine, and a younger brother, Albert Daniel, called A.D. The children were raised in a very stern household where Daddy King often used the strap on his sons. Grandmother Williams, whom the children called Mama, often spent a great deal of time with the boys after their strappings, sometimes going to her room, as she did not agree with the Reverend King's use of the strap. M.L. was 15 when he entered college and 18 when he preached his first sermon. Though he struggled with choosing a profession, he eventually determined that his role as a minister provided the best way to reach people with his beliefs concerning changes in race relations. The event presented in this script is M.L.'s first encounter with racial discrimination. Although based on a factual event, this script replaces Daddy King with Mama in order to introduce her caring, loving character as it balanced his home environment. Also, in the material available on this event, M.L.'s friend is referred to simply as a playmate. To make the playmate more real, he has been given the name Eddie. The term *discrimination* may need to be explained before reading this script so the students understand its relevance to the story.

STAGING

Center stage is the King kitchen, where all of the dialogue takes place. The Narrator should stand to the side of the room or in the back so attention is not drawn away from the center of the performance area. As the opening narration begins, Mother Dear should be in place. M.L., and later Mama, should enter from opposite sides of the staging area, because M.L. comes in from outside and Mama is already elsewhere in the house. Although there is no need for props in this script, a table, three chairs, and some typical kitchen objects would make the staging area more interesting. M.L. should carry a notebook or textbook as he comes home from school.

CHARACTERS

Narrator, Mother Dear, M.L., and Mama.

A Child's March to a Dream

Narrator:

Martin Luther King, Jr., was called M.L. by his family and friends. When he was five years old, his mother tried to enroll him in school early, as he was very bright. However, on his fifth birthday, he couldn't help bragging at school about his ability to blow out all five candles on his birthday cake at one time. He was promptly sent home. After his first day of school the next year, an excited M.L. ran to his friend's home, where the two boys talked about their day. When his friend's mother came to the door, she told M.L. that he and Eddie could no longer play together because M.L. was "colored." This was the first time M.L. encountered discrimination. M.L. ran home, crying.

Mother Dear:

M.L., what is wrong? Why are you crying?

M.L.:

She said I couldn't play with Eddie anymore 'cause I'm colored.

Mother Dear:

Who told you that?

M.L.:

Eddie's mother. She said we couldn't play together because I'm colored and Eddie's white. What does she mean, Mother?

Mother Dear:

M.L., I am sorry.

M.L.:

What's colored?

Mother Dear:

It is a term some people use when they are talking about people who have ancestors from Africa. Our ancestors are from Africa, so we are often called colored. Eddie's ancestors are from Europe and they are called white. It is a way of naming a different race or ethnic group.

M.L.:

Is being colored bad? Is that why I can't play with Eddie anymore?

Mother Dear:

No, M.L. Being of a different race is not bad, but it does cause problems between people sometimes. Right now it is causing a problem for you and Eddie.

M.L.:
Is that why Eddie and I go to a different school, 'cause of race?

Mother Dear:
Yes, it is.

M.L.:
Why do they want to keep us apart?

Mother Dear:
Because some people believe it is all right to discriminate against others.

Mama:
My, my. What a serious discussion after your first day at school. M.L., have you been crying?

M.L.:
Yes, Mama. Eddie's mother said we couldn't be friends anymore 'cause I'm colored. That's not fair, Mama.

Mama:
No, it's not, M.L. But I am afraid you are going to find out that there will be a lot of things in your life that are not fair.

M.L.:
Because I'm colored and 'cause of discrimination? Why is there discrimination?

Mama:
M.L., that's a very long story, but I'll try to help your mother tell you about it. Alberta, what have you told him so far?

Mother Dear:
Really nothing, Mother, except where our ancestors and Eddie's ancestors came from.

Mama:
M.L., many years ago, some Europeans went into Africa and kidnapped people. They brought many of them to the United States.

M.L.:
Kidnapped! Why would anyone do that?

Mama:

Some people in the United States had very big homes and plantations. They needed a lot of people to work in their homes and fields. Some Europeans kidnapped Africans and then sold them to the plantation owners or other people who needed help.

Mother Dear:

Once the Africans were sold to the white people, they owned the Africans and called them slaves. As slaves they had to do as the white people told them.

M.L.:

What happened to the people when they were slaves?

Mama:

Some were worked very hard by their owners. Some slaves were even beaten. Other slaves were treated better, and some were even freed by their owners. It all depended on what the owner was like.

M.L.:

Why didn't they run away from their mean owners?

Mother Dear:

If they got caught, they would be beaten badly or killed. If they didn't get caught, some of the owners would hurt their wives or children who were left behind.

M.L.:

Why were some owners mean to their slaves?

Mama:

Some people just didn't know how to treat other people nicely. Also, because they owned the slaves, some people thought they had the right to do with them as they pleased. Other owners were afraid of the Africans because they spoke a different language, had different customs, and looked different.

M.L.:

We're not slaves. How did it change?

Mother Dear:

There was a war between the people in the North, who wanted slavery stopped, and the people of the South, who had the slaves. When this war, called the Civil War, was over, so was slavery. The slaves were freed.

M.L.:

Well, if they were freed, how come I can't play with Eddie?

Mama:
The war freed the slaves, but it didn't change the fear of some whites about blacks. A lot of laws were passed to keep whites and blacks segregated—that means apart, M.L.

M.L.:
You mean like Eddie and I going to different schools?

Mother Dear:
Exactly. Some people were afraid of others who were different. But instead of learning how to get along, they passed laws that kept us from being friends. That's why Eddie's mother said you couldn't be friends anymore. Because the law says you have to go to different schools, Eddie's new friends will be white and yours will be black. His mother doesn't want him to have problems because you're black, so she decided to keep you apart all of the time.

M.L.:
But that's not fair. Eddie and I were always best friends. Why can't it change so we can stay best friends?

Mama:
There are a lot of people who are trying to make things better between the whites and blacks. Your Daddy King is one of them. He is working hard, but change comes slowly because it has to come from within a person. It is not as easy to change a person's heart as it is to pass a law.

M.L.:
Can I help Daddy King?

Mama:
Yes, you can, M.L. But first, there are some things you need to do. You have to decide for yourself that you can change things. Then you have to get a good education so you can understand why things are as they are now. You need to understand that you are just as important and good as anyone else is. Finally, when you are ready to help your Daddy King change things, you have to understand how he is doing it.

M.L.:
What do you mean? How is Daddy King making changes?

Mother Dear:
Daddy King is changing things peacefully, by example. He may get mad, but he never hits another person, nor does he destroy property. He leads people to a change of heart through his actions and words. Because he wants things to change for the better for everyone, he doesn't do things to make people mad at him or hate him. He does things in such a way that people will respect him and want to know him better.

M.L.:

That's what I am going to do, too. Then maybe someday Eddie and I can be friends again.

Narrator:

This was not M.L.'s only experience with discrimination. But it took only one experience to make M.L. realize discrimination was wrong, and he wanted it to change. It was while he was working toward that change that Martin Luther King, Jr.'s life was abruptly ended by a gunshot at the hands of an assassin. Today, his family continues to work toward ending discrimination in the United States.

Chinese New Year

A Special Invitation for Tommy*

BACKGROUND INFORMATION

In China, the Chinese New Year falls on the second new moon after the winter solstice. Although many Chinese Americans have adopted the modern custom of celebrating New Year's on the first of January, they also enjoy celebrating as their ancestors did. The Chinese New Year celebration lasts 15 days, beginning with Yuan Tan. The preparations begin weeks before, with a massive housecleaning and much cooking. As a rule, the families celebrate among themselves and do not ask others in. However, to teach about the Chinese New Year, in this script the Chang family will break with that tradition and invite their son's best friend, Tommy. The events in this story parallel the events of a typical Chinese New Year celebration.

STAGING

The Narrator should be positioned to one side of the staging area, either standing at a podium or sitting. The scenes between the two boys should take place on the other side of the stage, and the scenes with the parents should take place in the center of the stage. All participants may sit or move as they feel comfortable.

CHARACTERS

Narrator, Tommy, Linn, Mr. Chang, and Mrs. Chang.

VOCABULARY

Pronunciation for the Chinese terms used in this story follows:

Yuan Tan	Yoo-an Tahn
Ya shui chien	Yah shoo-ee chee-en
Sze Tse	Zee Tsee

*Information on the Chinese New Year was obtained from Lois S. Johnson, *Happy New Year Around the World* (New York: Rand McNally, 1966).

EXTENSION ACTIVITIES

This story lends itself easily to several art projects and activities. Students could make paper lanterns. Traditional lanterns include the following shapes: cylinders, balls, cubes, houses, cars, fans, animals, airplanes, and Chinese pagodas. Certain shapes may be more difficult to make in the early grades, so children can draw these as pictures on the lanterns and then cut the slits necessary to allow the light out. Most art books contain a basic lantern design.

Dragon making provides other project opportunities. Each child could make a small dragon by painting the sections of a cardboard egg carton. The individual egg cups should be separated, yielding 12 cups. Turn the cups upside down and paint them in varying colors and designs. Once the cups are dry, punch holes in two sides of each cup and thread the cups together using string or pipe cleaners. If the students are younger, pipe cleaners will be easier for them to thread and knot (or, in this case, twist). The first cup will represent the dragon's head; students can glue pieces of construction paper to it to represent the dragon's facial features.

A very ambitious teacher may want to make a large "class-size" dragon, using large decorated and painted cardboard boxes for dragon sections. Students can wear the boxes, holding hands as the dragon moves so that the sections appear to be attached. An elaborate dragon can also be made using a tie-dyed sheet, which students can line up and move under. A tie-dyed pillowcase represents the head of the dragon. The first student in line (representing the dragon's head) should stand upright; the others should walk bent over, representing the dragon's body. Students could also make individual dragon masks; with these and the large, class-size dragon, the children could have a parade.

The script also discusses traditional flowers and colors used to decorate the home for Chinese New Year. Making the various flowers, which the children can then take home to their mothers, is a fun way to spend art time. Although narcissus and peach or plum blossoms are the traditional flowers of Chinese New Year, it may be difficult to obtain a good visual example for the children to copy from. A daffodil can serve as a guide for the narcissus, as the flowers are of the same genus. To make a narcissus, trace a pattern onto white construction paper. The pink to deep reddish purple tree blossoms can be made from colored tissue paper and construction paper. Blossoms in bud form can be created by winding tissue paper around a pencil eraser and gluing these "buds" onto a small twig for a more authentic appearance. Small open blossoms can be made from construction paper by gluing semicircular petals around a small white or yellow center.

Another extension activity might be a writing lesson in which children make up wishes. After writing them down on slips of paper, students could attempt to wrap the small papers around coins. If this proves too difficult, they could simply exchange the wish slips with each other. Children love to slip messages into each other's desks, and what better message could there be than a wish?

A Special Invitation for Tommy

Narrator:

Tommy Webber meets Linn Chang every day in front of Linn's house to walk to school. They have been best friends since kindergarten. The Changs moved into their home just before Linn started kindergarten. Linn told Tommy that his family moved there so he could go to this school. His parents knew some of the teachers there and felt it was a good school for Linn. On the day that the boys met each other, they became good friends. They always went to school together, played at each other's houses, and often invited each other to very special events. This year Tommy will get a very special invitation from the Changs.

Tommy:

Linn, aren't you ready for school yet?

Linn:

Just a minute. I almost forgot something very important.

Tommy:

What is so important that it couldn't wait until after school?

Linn:

This. *(He hands Tommy an envelope)*

Tommy:

What is this?

Linn:

Open it and see.

Tommy:

Oh, Linn, this is wonderful! Am I really invited to Yuan Tan?

Linn:

Yes. Mother and Father said I could ask you if I wanted to. You know it is an honor that you are invited, don't you?

Tommy:

No. What do you mean?

Linn:

It is not our ancestors' custom to have people who are not family members at our home to celebrate Yuan Tan. It is a family celebration. But I told my mother and father that you are just like my brother and I wanted you to come. They thought it over for a long time and then said it would be okay. But I have to teach you certain things before you come.

Tommy:

Why?

Linn:

Because there are certain things that we always do on this day, and I don't want you to make a mistake.

Tommy:

Like what?

Linn:

For one thing, you will have to take off your shoes when you come into the house.

Tommy:

Why?

Linn:

My mother has been very busy cleaning the house. She does that to get all of the dirt from last year out of the house so we will have good luck. We have to remember to take off our shoes when we go in so we do not track in any dirt.

Tommy:

Is that what she has been doing? I thought it was just spring housecleaning like my mother does.

Linn:

I guess it is like that. She has been very careful to get everything cleaned and repainted if it needs it.

Tommy:

What does she do once she gets the house cleaned?

Linn:

She will begin to decorate. That is why you will see so many flowers in the house, as well as red papers and pictures hanging around. Red means good luck and happiness, so you will see a lot of it everywhere. The candles will be red, too.

Tommy:

Why do you have many flowers?

Linn:

That is part of our tradition. Each color and type of flower stands for something important. Like the white narcissus. It means good fortune. Pink blossoms of the peach or plum tree mean long life. Everything you see when you come in the house has a meaning and is special for us.

Tommy:

Do I have to remember all of this?

Linn:

No, but I want you to understand it. That way you won't be afraid of anything or think something is so different you do not want to stay for the whole day.

Tommy:

Okay. Look, I'll put this invitation in my pocket so I don't loose it, and you can tell me more about the day on our way home. Do you think we will really have a math test today?

Linn:

Probably. It shouldn't be that hard, though. You are good in math, Tommy.

Tommy:

I know. I just don't like to take tests. They make me nervous. Guess we'd better get inside. That's the second bell.

Narrator:

While Tommy and Linn spend the day in class, Linn's mother is preparing for the arrival of Yuan Tan. Besides cleaning and decorating, she has been busy cooking and preparing for the ritual of sending the Kitchen God to heaven. It is the Kitchen God's job to report on how the family has behaved during the past year. An image of a man has been in place in the kitchen all year. This image is placed on an altar along with sweets so he will remember the sweet things the family did during the year. This afternoon, when Linn comes home from school, they will set the altar on fire and set off fireworks. As the flames and smoke drift to heaven, the fireworks scare away any evil spirits that may be around.

Tommy:

Linn, slow down. Why are you in such a hurry to get home? I thought you were going to tell me more about the New Year celebrations.

Linn:
I will. In fact, today we have one of the many celebrations that happen between now and Yuan Tan. I don't want to be late.

Tommy:
I thought Yuan Tan was the only celebration of the Chinese New Year.

Linn:
Oh, no! But many of the smaller celebrations are ones that come down from our ancestors and would probably seem silly to you.

Tommy:
Why?

Linn:
Because they are very old customs and not like anything that is done in America.

Tommy:
Well, tell me about the one that you are doing today. I'd like to know about it even if it does seem silly to me.

Linn:
Okay. You know that picture that hangs in our kitchen?

Tommy:
The one of your grandfather?

Linn:
Well, yes. Except it isn't of my grandfather. It is a picture of our Kitchen God.

Tommy:
Your Kitchen God?

Linn:
Yes. Every Chinese family's kitchen has an image of a Kitchen God hung in it. This god watches over our family, and seven days before the great celebration, his image is burned. He then goes to heaven, where he reports on our family's behavior. Then, on New Year's Eve, a new image is placed in the kitchen. This Kitchen God will watch over us for the next year, until it is time for him to complete his mission.

Tommy:
Wow! Here all the time I thought you were putting up different pictures of your grandfathers! I am not sure I would want a Kitchen God in my house.

Linn:

Why not?

Tommy:

I'd have to really watch what I did and said all the time. That wouldn't be much fun.

Linn:

But that is just the point, Tommy. With the Kitchen God in place, you do watch what you do and say. It helps you remember to be a good person all of the time, not just sometimes.

Tommy:

I guess so. Do you think I could stay for the celebration today?

Linn:

I don't think so. My parents agreed to the New Year's Day celebration because we are almost like brothers. I don't think they are ready for me to have you at all of our celebrations. Maybe next year they will let you come for this one, too. It is difficult for them to change their ways and ideas very quickly. So I'll ask them to let you come next year, okay?

Tommy:

Sure. Well, you have a good time at your celebration. I'll see you tomorrow. Bye.

Narrator:

For the next six days Linn's mother and father are very busy preparing for the New Year's Day celebration. Everything must be cooked ahead because no one can use a knife on New Year's Day. It is feared one might cut the luck of the new year while using a knife. It is also the time to settle old debts. No one goes into the new year owing money. According to Chinese custom, all debts must be paid by the stroke of midnight on the last day of the year. In China, if you do not pay your debts, a one-candle lantern is hung at your door by the person you owe money to. If you owe many people money, many lanterns may be left burning at your door. Imagine how embarrassing that would be for you and your family. Finally, New Year's Day arrives. When Linn awakens, he finds Ya Shui Chien under his pillow. Ya Shui Chien are coins that have been wrapped in red paper. On each sheet of paper is written a different wish in gold or silver ink. Each wish represents something good that the parents hope will happen for their children during the new year.

Linn:

Father, thank you for the wonderful wishes. If they all come true, I will have an exciting year.

Mr. Chang:
You are welcome, Linn. Come, it is time for us to give thanks for all that we have and to remember our ancestors and how important they have been in our lives.

Narrator:
After this ceremony, the family spends the day together. In China, family members spend this day at their grandparents' home. Because Chinese families are very large, there are always many people at the home of the grandparents. However, Linn and his parents have no other family in America. That is why the Changs decided Linn could invite Tommy.

Mrs. Chang:
Linn, it is almost time for Tommy to arrive. Do you have the table ready for all of us?

Mr. Chang:
I think Linn has had the table ready for the last hour. You are quite excited about having Tommy come, aren't you?

Linn:
Oh, yes, Father. Not only will I have someone my age to play the games with, I will get to teach Tommy more about our ancestors' customs.

Mr. Chang:
What have you been telling Tommy so far?

Linn:
Everything! Every day that there has been a special event, I have told him about it. He wants to know what we do as we celebrate the new year.

Mrs. Chang:
How does Tommy act when you tell him about some of our customs?

Linn:
Interested. And he asks many questions so that he will understand things better.

Mrs. Chang:
Doesn't he find some of what you tell him strange?

Linn:
No. He says it helps him understand how we are different, and how we are so much alike. He has never laughed at anything I have told him. I think he really just wants to learn about me because we are such good friends.

Mr. Chang:
You are very lucky to have such a good friend. You must treasure that because many people you meet will not be so understanding.

Linn:
Oh, I know that, Father. But Tommy is special. That is why I wanted him to come today. He will really enjoy the day, just you wait and see. Oh, I think I hear him coming now. Tommy, come in.

Tommy:
Just a minute, I need to take off my shoes. Here, can you hold these?

Linn:
What have you got in this paper?

Tommy:
Something for your mother. Okay, I'll take that now.

Linn:
Mother. Father. Tommy is here.

Mr. Chang:
Welcome to our home, Tommy, and may you have happiness in this new year.

Tommy:
Thank you, Sir. And thank you for asking me. I could hardly sleep last night, waiting for this afternoon to get here. Mrs. Chang, these are for you.

Mrs. Chang:
Why, Tommy, thank you. They are such beautiful flowers.

Tommy:
Linn told me that you like to have many flowers on New Year's Day. Especially red ones and the white narcissus because they represent good fortune and good luck. And that is what I wish you, all of you. That and happiness, also.

Mrs. Chang:
Well, thank you, Tommy, for your wishes and your flowers. It is very nice to have you join us. It is almost time to eat. Are you hungry, Tommy?

Tommy:
Oh, yes, Mrs. Chang, I sure am. I was very careful to eat only a little breakfast. Linn has told me so much about all of the cooking you have been doing that I can hardly wait to try everything!

Narrator:

Tommy was not disappointed in the grand meal Mrs. Chang had fixed. There was a whole roasted pig, chicken, duck, and fish. Plus, they had fried rice, shrimp, cabbage, some fruit, and so many sweets for dessert that it was hard for Tommy to decide what to eat. After the family finished the meal, Mr. Chang told Tommy and Linn stories about his family, still in China. Then they played some games together. At the end of the evening, Tommy got another surprise from the Changs.

Mr. Chang:

Tommy, on our New Year's Day, everyone celebrates his or her birthday. Today, everyone is one year older, even if his or her birthday is not until next fall. Also, we give our children Ya Shui Chien as gifts. I want to wish you a happy birthday also, and to give you some Ya Shui Chien.

Tommy:

Why, thank you, Mr. Chang. Linn told me about these special coins. I did not expect to get any! Thank you.

Mr. Chang:

Tommy, Linn told us that he has been telling you all about our celebrations. He also said that you have been a very good learner. After spending today with you, I understand why my son feels you are like a brother to him. Tommy, for the next 15 days there will be many different parades and events as we continue to celebrate the new year. I would like you to join us for those celebrations, if it is all right with your parents. But if you cannot join us every day, I do hope you can join us for the Festival of Lanterns.

Tommy:

Oh, thank you, again, Mr. Chang. I would like to go to all of the parades and events with your family. I am sure it will be all right with my parents. Will I get to see the lion? I forget what Linn said it was called.

Mrs. Chang:

Sze Tse. Yes, I am sure you will see Sze Tse many different times over the next few days.

Tommy:

I guess it is time for me to go home. I am very honored that you have invited me to be part of your family for the new year celebrations, Mr. and Mrs. Chang. I will see you tomorrow, then. Thank you again. Bye, Linn.

Narrator:

For the next 14 days, Tommy and Linn, with Linn's parents, attended many parades. On the fifteenth day, Tommy joined the Changs as they lit lanterns and followed a huge dragon through the streets of Chinatown. Tommy had a wonderful time. Not only did he get to spend a great deal of time with the Changs, but he learned how important a family's ancestors could be to that family's beliefs. Tommy was sad to see the new year celebrations end, but Mr. Chang invited him to join them next year, even to the celebration of the Kitchen God's departure.

Groundhog Day

From Beside a Tunnel

BACKGROUND INFORMATION

Most people observe February 2 as Groundhog Day, although the date was originally a religious holiday. It began as a pagan celebration featuring a candlelight procession to purify and invigorate the fields before they were planted. It later became a Christian holiday, Candlemas Day, marking the presentation of Christ in the temple and the purification of Mary.

On Groundhog Day, tradition has it, the woodchuck would emerge from hibernation and look for his shadow. (In some parts of Europe, the badger or bear is the weather prognosticator.) If he saw it, he burrowed for six more weeks, indicating more bad winter weather to come. If there was no shadow, he would not burrow, signifying spring was on its way. The lack of sun indicated a good planting season ahead, whereas sunshine was thought to portend harsh weather and poor planting.

The earliest reference to Groundhog Day in the United States was made in 1841 by James L. Morris of Morgantown, Pennsylvania, who referred to it as a German holiday.

STAGING

The Narrator should stand to the left of the staging area; the others should sit stage center. There are no props, nor is there any movement in this script.

CHARACTERS

Narrator, June, Adam, Ernie, and Cathy.

From Beside a Tunnel

Narrator:

In Punxsutawney, Pennsylvania, it is almost sunrise. Hiding in the bushes around a groundhog hole are four friends. They are waiting to see if the groundhog will come out of his hole and see his shadow. If he sees his shadow, there will be more bad winter weather coming. If the groundhog does not see his shadow, the weather will be very nice.

June:

How much longer do we have to wait here?

Adam:

Shhh! You don't want him to hear you. He may get scared and not come out of his hole.

Ernie:

Adam's right. Can't you and Cathy ever be patient?

Cathy:

We can be as patient as you are; it's just that it's cold sitting on the ground.

Ernie:

I told you to wear warm clothes and bring something to sit on.

Cathy:

But you didn't tell us we'd be sitting here all day.

Adam:

We won't be here all day, Cathy. See, the sun is just beginning to come up. It won't be long now before the groundhog comes out of that hole.

June:

How do you know that?

Adam:

Because it's February 2nd. Everyone knows that animals hibernate during the coldest part of winter. When it begins to warm up, they come out of hibernation to test the weather.

Cathy:

What do you mean by "test the weather"?

Ernie:
They come out to see if it has begun to warm up enough to leave their homes. If not, they hibernate for six more weeks.

June:
How can they tell if it's time or not?

Adam:
By instinct.

Cathy:
What's instinct?

Adam:
Just something they know. Kinda like knowing when it's time to eat 'cause you feel hungry. Only with the groundhog, it's knowing whether it's time to leave his burrow. Look, there's the sunrise! It sure is pretty.

June:
Well, I don't see much sun. Is that good or bad?

Ernie:
Depends on whether you're a farmer or not.

Cathy:
What's farming got to do with the groundhog?

Ernie:
Well, farmers used to think that if the groundhog saw his shadow and went back into his burrow, it would be harder to get the ground ready to plant.

June:
What did they have to do to get the ground ready? Didn't they just run a big machine?

Adam:
Back then they had to plow by hand or with a horse-drawn plow. It was hard to do if the ground was still frozen. I guess now machines make it easier, even if the ground is frozen.

Ernie:
Shhh! Look!

Cathy:
It's the groundhog! What's he doing?

Adam:
Just standing there looking around. I guess he's waiting to see if he sees his shadow.

Cathy:
How long will he wait?

Adam:
I don't know. I've never done this before.

Ernie:
He won't wait long. Look, he's walking away from his burrow a little bit! I guess he doesn't see his shadow.

June:
How do you know?

Ernie:
Because if he did, he would go right back down into his burrow. Well, that's good news, huh?

June:
What's good news?

Adam:
He's not going back into his burrow.

June:
Why's that good news?

Adam:
Didn't you pay attention last time? If he goes back into his burrow, the weather will remain cold, and maybe a lot more snow will fall. If he stays out, like he is today, the weather will be mild or nice. It means the worst of the winter weather is over.

Cathy:
I bet the farmers are glad about that. Can they farm earlier this year?

Ernie:
I suppose some of them will, if it isn't too rainy.

June:
So, we can still have bad weather?

Adam:
If you call rain bad weather. I'd rather have a little rain than snow. Rain goes away faster.

Cathy:
Is this it? Is it over?

Adam:
I guess so. It was really neat, huh?

Cathy:
If you say so. I just want to go home and warm up.

Ernie:
Well, thanks to the groundhog, you know it will be warming up every day from now on.

June:
That's great. Are we going now?

Adam:
Okay, let's go. Next year, Ernie, let's come out here by ourselves!

Narrator:
Watching the groundhog in Punxsutawney, Pennsylvania, has become a major event. Each year people watch as the groundhog at Gobbler's Knob makes its way out to test the weather. If you get up early enough, you can even watch the event on television. Just like the people in Punxsutawney, you'll get to see if the groundhog, called Punxsutawney Phil, stays outside or goes back into his burrow to hibernate for another six weeks.

Esther's Lacy Valentine

BACKGROUND INFORMATION

Although the precise origins of Valentine's Day are uncertain, the first valentine made in the United States can be traced to Esther Howland. After receiving a lacy valentine from a friend in England in 1847, Esther decided to begin her own card business. Not only was it one of the first businesses in the United States run by a woman, it was also very successful. Before long, her line included Christmas cards, May baskets, and other holiday favors, bringing an annual income of $100,000, approximately $538,000 today. Although her items could be as expensive as $10, or $54 today, for a May basket, the popularity of her valentines grew. It wasn't long before other companies began to manufacture valentines, both serious and comic.

STAGING

The Narrator should stand to one side of the staging area. Esther and her father should sit far to the other side, close to the front of the performance area. The other readers should sit center stage and somewhat farther back. As Esther's discussion with her father ends and the discussion with her friends begins, she should move to the area where her friends are. Remember to place an empty chair among the group so that Esther has somewhere to sit once she joins them.

CHARACTERS

Narrator, Esther, Mr. Howland, Margaret, Alice, and Martha.

Esther's Lacy Valentine

Narrator:

It is the year 1847. Esther Howland and her father, a merchant, live in Worcester, Massachusetts. Although he sells mainly writing supplies and books in his store, he is one of the first merchants to import valentines. The valentines he stocks are rather plain, with simple verses inside of them. However, a valentine Esther receives from a friend in England will change all of that forever.

Esther:

Papa, look! Have you ever seen anything like this in your whole life? I don't believe I have ever seen such a beautiful valentine—all of the lace and the bright colors. Papa, these are the kind you should be selling, not those plain cards over there.

Mr. Howland:

Where did that come from?

Esther:

From Cousin Mary in England, Papa. Surely you can get some from your suppliers to sell here, too. Everyone would want to send these beautiful valentines. I can't wait to show this one to my friends.

Narrator:

Her father imported the new valentines for the next season, and Esther's prediction came true. The new valentines were quite popular. Esther was so intrigued by them, she began to create her own.

Mr. Howland:

Esther, I do believe your cards are even more beautiful than the ones I have ordered from England. If you can make several of them for me, I will try to sell them next year.

Esther:

Oh, Papa. I am just making these for my friends. You can't seriously expect me to make more of them to sell.

Mr. Howland:

Esther, I know my customers and I know cards. Yours are better than any I have had in the store. I'll tell you what. You make just a few for me to set out and we will take orders. If you are right and no one is interested, then you will not have spent a great deal of time for nothing. But if I am right, you are going to be a very busy young lady.

Esther:
Papa, I think you have valentines in your eyes. But I will give you these two. When it gets closer to Valentine's Day, you can set them out, if it will make you happy.

Narrator:
When January came, Mr. Howland put out Esther's valentines. He began to take orders for them. Esther was pleased to know that people liked her cards better than the ones from England. As the season came to an end, several people placed orders ahead for the next year. Because she had so much time to prepare the valentines, they were even more elaborate and beautiful than the first ones she had completed. Mr. Howland decided to buy all of the supplies from Europe he could and let her create cards all year long. The following January, when the supplies came in from England, Esther did not see any boxes of valentines.

Esther:
Papa, where are the boxes of valentines you usually get from England?

Mr. Howland:
Esther, all year long you have been assembling one valentine after another. With each of them, you become more and more creative. Why should I import valentines when yours are so much better?

Esther:
But Papa, I have not made many extra valentines. Most of these are for the orders I already have.

Mr. Howland:
Just give me a few to put out on display. I will take orders, and you can make them up as they come in.

Esther:
But Papa, what if I run out of time or supplies?

Mr. Howland:
Esther, you will not run out of supplies. I have seen to that. Maybe your friends could help you if you get a lot of orders and are rushed for time.

Esther:
Papa, I hope you know what you are doing!

Narrator:
By the end of January, Esther had more orders than she could keep up with. After sitting up night after night working on the valentines, she decided to take her father's suggestion and ask her friends to help.

Esther:

Margaret, Martha, and Alice, I am glad you came. I need your help. Papa put out some of my valentines and took orders for more. He had no idea what he was getting me into. I have to make hundreds of valentines in the next 20 days. Do you think you can help me get them done?

Margaret:

What is it you want us to do?

Esther:

For now, all we have to do is remake the designs he has on display in the store. If everyone takes a job, it will go faster.

Alice:

What do you mean?

Esther:

If you cut out the valentine shapes, and Martha glues on all of the flowers and other small decorations, and Margaret paints on the leaves and stems, I'll write the verses. This will speed up the process. As each of us finishes her part of the card, she can pass that card on to the next person and then start another card. This way no one has to try to make the whole card by herself. Will you help me?

Martha:

I am willing to try. I don't know if I can do the things just as you did them, but I will do my best. You'll help, won't you Margaret?

Margaret:

Why not? It could be really fun! And it does give us an excuse to spend lots of our time together!

Narrator:

With a great deal of help from her friends, Esther was able to fill all of the orders she had for valentines that year. Learning from this experience, Esther hired her friends, and they began making valentines earlier for the next year. As her valentines became more and more popular, Esther's needs far exceeded the ability of human hands to cut and decorate the cards. Esther finally had to buy machinery to do some of the work so that she could keep up with the orders. Her valentines were so popular that other companies began to copy her ideas and produce large numbers of valentines, too. Esther's valentine business was one of the first businesses in the United States run by a woman. With the success of her valentines, Esther decided to enhance her business and make Christmas cards and May baskets. It was not long until Esther had taken a simple valentine and made it into a $100,000-a-year business.

Presidents' Day

Abe, a Father's Story

BACKGROUND INFORMATION

This story is based on known facts about President Lincoln and his relationship with his sons. The dialogue is my own version of events. Reverend Gurley was Lincoln's pastor and did meet with the president on many issues while Lincoln was in Washington. He also presided over Lincoln's funeral and entombment in Springfield, Illinois.

STAGING

The Narrator should stand to the left of the performance area. All other readers should sit on stools or chairs in the center of the staging area. If you wish to avoid characters' entering and exiting, have readers stand and move forward to present their dialogue, then return to their seats while others read.

CHARACTERS

Narrator, Tad, Abe, Reverend Gurley, and Mary.

Abe, a Father's Story

Narrator:

When the Lincolns lived in Springfield, Illinois, they were a happy family. Abe traveled a lot as a lawyer, but when he was home, he spent a great deal of time with his sons, Tad and Willie. The boys shared a dog with their neighbors, as they were not allowed to have one of their own. When Abe was elected president of the United States, it was necessary to leave Springfield and move to Washington, D.C. The final day of packing was hard for Tad, as he was leaving behind so much that he cared about.

Tad:

But Daddy, why can't we take the dog with us?

Abe:

Son, you know how your mother feels about animals in the house, so it wouldn't be fair to take him with us and make him live outside. Besides, he really isn't our dog.

Tad:

But Daddy, I'm gonna miss him. I don't want to be alone.

Abe:

Tad, you won't be alone. Willie will be there. So will your mother and I. There'll be a lot of new people to meet and know. You'll never be alone.

Tad:

Yes, I will. There won't be anyone just for me.

Abe:

I'll tell you what, Tad. When we get to Washington, I will buy you a pony.

Tad:

A pony! Really? You will really buy me a pony?

Abe:

I said I would, Tad. Now, you get that frown off of your face and help pack your things, okay?

Tad:

Sure, Daddy. A real pony! I can hardly wait to get to Washington.

Narrator:

True to his word, Abe bought Tad his own pony. The boys loved riding the pony around the lawn of the White House. Many people criticized Abe for buying the pony. They thought he spoiled his sons, but they did not know of his promise to Tad. Abe was also criticized for the freedom the boys seemed to have in the White House.

Abe spent many hours discussing his problems with his pastor at the Presbyterian church he attended in Washington. Reverend Gurley knew more about Abe and the problems of the government than most of the members of Congress and Mr. Lincoln's staff. It was not unusual for Abe to leave his office at the White House and show up unexpectedly at Reverend Gurley's office.

Abe:

Excuse me, Reverend. Do you have a few minutes to spare me?

Rev. Gurley:

Mr. Lincoln, come in. Of course I can spare you time, all the time you need. What seems to be the problem? You look as if you've lost your best friend.

Abe:

Well, Reverend, it may come to that. It seems there is quite a commotion about my boys. During the last couple of weeks, I've let them sit under my desk and quietly play while I held various meetings. Seems some of my political friends feel that this is improper.

Rev. Gurley:

Have they told you this, or is it just rumor?

Abe:

I have heard it from a very reliable person on my staff, Reverend. If the boys were a bother, I'd understand people complaining. But my children just want to be with me. My time is in such demand, I get only a few minutes a day with the boys, at best. They're growing up so fast and there's so little time to spend with them. When we lived in Springfield, I could spend hours with them, playing games and reading. Now, I'm lucky if I pass them in the halls on some days. They complain that they miss their daddy. And frankly, I miss them.

Rev. Gurley:

I understand how you feel, Mr. Lincoln. Children do grow up quickly. Perhaps your problem lies more with the men you have on your staff and in your committees than it does with your boys.

Abe:

What do you mean?

Rev. Gurley:

Mr. Lincoln, if they had the same concern and love for their sons and daughters, I am sure they would not be as critical about your sons sitting under your desk. What do the boys do while sitting there?

Abe:

They play with their small toys. Sometimes I can feel them untying my shoelaces and retying them. Fortunately for me, I haven't had to walk away from my desk with my shoes tied together. Can you imagine the stories the staff would tell if I fell flat on my face because my shoes had been tied together?

Rev. Gurley:

Now that's a sight to consider! Mr. Lincoln, I think you should ignore the complaints of these people. With all the concerns of war facing us, I think this is of little importance. You're doing the best you can do to keep your family life together in very difficult times. If they were my sons, I'd let them play under my desk all they wanted. If that keeps them happy, and you enjoy knowing they're there during those difficult discussions, I wouldn't let the talk stop me at all. After all, Mr. Lincoln, our time on earth is short, and we should use it as wisely as we can. I can't think of a better way for you to satisfy both your sons' needs and the country's.

Abe:

Thank you, Reverend Gurley. It is always good to come and talk to you. You can always calm my fears and clear up my confusion. I'll get out of your way now. See you Sunday.

Narrator:

Abe never did make his sons move from under the desk. Whenever they were in the office visiting their father and a meeting was to begin, they would quietly scoot beneath the desk just to stay close to him. Although the government officials may have become accustomed to seeing the boys under the desk, they still did not like it. Neither did they—or Abe's wife, Mary—approve of the nanny goats Abe bought Tad. The pony was one thing, but the nanny goats were the final straw for Mary.

Mary:

Abe, how could you buy Tad nanny goats, of all things?

Abe:

Now Mary, why all of the fuss? Just think of the value they have. Why, they can cut the gardener's work in half just by grazing on the lawn. He can spend more time on the flowers and other chores he never seems to get to.

Mary:

Abe, the gardener is not the point! Nanny goats do not belong at the White House. And so help me if anyone ever finds out that Tad brings them upstairs to sleep with him. Why, we'll be the laughing stock of Washington.

Abe:

Oh, Mary, really—it's no big deal. If you had let the boys have a dog, maybe Tad wouldn't be taking the nanny goats to bed with him.

Mary:

Naturally you would take Tad's side in this. You're always taking the boys' side in everything. I tell you, Abe, no man in his right mind lets his son have nanny goats in his bed.

Abe:

Mary, I am in my right mind and I will not tell Tad he has to keep his nanny goats outside if he doesn't want to. They're not in your bed, so I don't know what the harm is.

Mary:

Mr. Lincoln, the harm is that you are the president of the United States and your son should not act like a common . . . common . . .

Abe:

Common farmer, Mary? Remember, I was a farmer. Granted, I didn't have a nanny goat in my bed, but we had goats, dogs, horses, and many other animals around our house. In spite of all of that, look where we are now, Mrs. Lincoln. I don't think nanny goats in Tad's bed are going to hurt him, or us, one bit.

Mary:

In other words, you are going to let him keep those nanny goats?

Abe:

Yes, I am, Mary. I'm going to let him have them and anything else he and Willie want that brings a smile to their sad little faces. Living here has not been easy. They have not been very happy, so I'll do whatever I can to make our time here easier. Even if that means nanny goats in Tad's bed.

Mary:

I shudder to think what the next thing you give them will be, just for a smile.

Abe:

My dear wife, I haven't even considered anything else yet. But I can assure you that whatever it is, as long as it works, that's all that matters.

Narrator:

As time continued to pass in Washington, the smiles on the faces of Abe's sons grew fewer and fewer, as did the smiles on the faces of most people in the United States. It was a terrible time in our history as the Civil War dragged on and so many lives were lost. Every death seemed to age Abe, but the hardest death of all for him to bear would be his son Willie's. This death not only took the smile from Abe's face, it took the spirit out of the family. As they faced the months after Willie's death, the Lincoln family found little to smile about. And Abe, the fun-loving father, became Abe, the heartbroken president.

Presidents' Day

The Other Life of a President

BACKGROUND INFORMATION

When celebrating Presidents' Day, most of us teach about George Washington as the first president. For me, deciding on a president to highlight was difficult; finally, I selected our third president, Thomas Jefferson. Like so many presidents, he had a law background that helped him as he worked his way through the early political system. Like all other presidents, he had a life apart from the presidency, in his case, a very difficult life. It is this other life that I will highlight, as I want to make readers aware that holding the office of president occupies a very brief—though very influential—period in a person's life. Beyond being president, those who have held this position have had other jobs, dreams, and a family life that are often overlooked. Therefore, this script will try to identify Thomas Jefferson as a person, as well as the third president. This script is written for older students in grade 6 and up.

This script may also be used as a springboard for class research on our various presidents. In researching the many facets of the president's job, students will get a better idea of the men we have elected to represent us. It is a good way for students to learn that our elected officials come from many walks of life and represent a vast array of beliefs and personal goals.

STAGING

The Narrator should sit or stand to one side of the staging area; the other readers can sit center stage. There will be no props for this reading. Unless students feel a need to enter and exit the stage, you may want to position the seats toward the back and have the readers step forward to present their lines and then return to their seats.

CHARACTERS

Narrator, Richard, Thomas, and James.

The Other Life of a President

Narrator:

When Thomas Jefferson was 14 years old, his father died. By this time Thomas had already learned to hunt, fish, farm, and read under his father's watchful eye. An accomplished horse rider, he was also able to dance and play the violin, chess, and cards. At age 15, he entered the College of William and Mary for two years. Here he learned little except to take on others' problems as if they were his own. At age 17 he began to study law, and at age 24 he was admitted to the bar. When the American Revolution broke out, Jefferson was a successful lawyer and a devoted husband and father. He was also an active member of the Virginia House of Burgesses. As the story opens, member Richard Lee of Virginia is enlisting Thomas's help in writing the Declaration of Independence.

Richard:

Now that we have engaged in a war to establish our desire to be independent from England, we need you to draft a document declaring our independence.

Thomas:

Not by myself, I hope. I do not want that responsibility on my shoulders alone.

Richard:

Of course not, Thomas. There will be a committee. It's only fair to everyone that this document be the result of several people's ideas. I just want you to do the final writing.

Thomas:

Why me?

Richard:

Because I know of no one else who has your background in writing such documents. You have been published on our need to have certain rights, and you have drafted resolutions that have been used to try to persuade the British to see our side of things. We need your broad base of knowledge and understanding of the people's needs to draft this document. You will do it, won't you?

Thomas:

If the rest of the Congress agrees with you, how can I refuse?

Richard:

Thank you, Thomas. I knew I could count on you. I will address the Congress tomorrow.

Narrator:

Although there were some minor changes to the original document that Jefferson presented to the Congress, the Declaration of Independence represented Jefferson's beliefs that people had certain rights. Once people were given these rights, they could use them to govern themselves fairly and successfully. He did more than write these beliefs down for others to live by: This was the way he lived his own life. For the next 20 years, Jefferson's life was a struggle, both politically and personally. In 1795, James Madison attempted to persuade Jefferson to run for the presidency.

Thomas:

James, to what do I owe the honor of your company on such a bitter night?

James:

Thomas, you see through me already?

Thomas:

I know you well enough, my old friend, to know you would not come all the way out here if you did not have something important on your mind. And knowing you as well as I do, that usually means you want something of me.

James:

I won't lie to you, Thomas. I do have something on my mind that I feel is very important and that I think you should consider.

Thomas:

What could that be, James?

James:

As you know, our country is in need of a strong, honest, and capable leader. Times have been so difficult since the war. It seems as if nothing is settled yet. I have been asked to convince you to run for our next president.

Thomas:

James, there is nothing in the world you could ask me that I would say no to but this. I don't have the energy to go back into the political ring. Every time I have been in a leading role in the past 20 years, it has caused me nothing but heartache. That mess when I was leader of the House of Delegates and governor of Virginia should have been enough of government for any man.

James:

But Thomas, everyone knows you did not betray our country. You were governor during a period of war, and your aides abandoned you. The investigation vindicated you.

Thomas:

But look what it cost me at the time! Then just a year later, I lost my wife, Martha. And I had yet to get over that when I let you talk me into becoming secretary of state. You said it would help me get over my grief. All it did was put me right back into the middle of that political mess. Everywhere I turned, I was perceived as being in opposition to the government. I don't like walking up mountains alone. No, James, no. You aren't going to talk me into running for president.

James:

Thomas, surely you don't like living out here at Monticello by yourself, do you? How much excitement can there be here?

Thomas:

That's just the point, James. There is no political excitement. That's the way I want to keep it. I like planting wheat. Why, I've got one of the largest grist mills in the area. And just last week my nail manufacturing concern doubled its business. Why do I need politics?

James:

You may not need politics, but the people need you. They need that man who wrote the Declaration. They need a leader who believes in them and in himself. Will you think about it, Thomas?

Thomas:

I'll think about it.

Narrator:

In 1796, Thomas Jefferson received 68 electoral votes to John Adams's 71. Jefferson became Adams's vice-president. In the election of 1800, Jefferson again ran for president but this time tied Aaron Burr with a total of 73 votes each. The election was turned over to the House of Representatives, and on March 4, 1801, Thomas Jefferson was elected the third president of the United States. It was not an easy time for him. In 1807, Jefferson returned to Monticello a tired, broke, and once again maligned man.

Thomas:

Have you come out here to apologize?

James:

I suppose you think I should?

Thomas:

I told you the presidency would cause me nothing but grief. Look at me. I am nearly broke. Once again, everyone thinks I have betrayed my country. My enemies have accused me of everything from cowardice to trying to subvert our youth with scientific studies that my critics say go against the word of God. Please, tell me you're here as a friend and that you don't have another scheme to get me back into politics.

James:

No, Thomas, I don't. I still feel you were the best person for the country. It's just that the country doesn't realize it. People are out for themselves, not for what is best for all of us. You would have been an unbelievable leader if they had let you lead. You were right. I just hoped you could turn things around. I'm sorry things went so badly for you. I never wanted you to be hurt further.

Thomas:

James, it's not your fault. I was drawn into thinking I could be that leader. I knew what my enemies were like. Heaven knows, the only thing that changed about them was their names. There's just that group of men out there who do not want us to succeed. I'm sorry if you feel I let you down. I did what I felt was best for the country, even though it cost me dearly.

James:

I know you did, Thomas. What are you planning to do now?

Thomas:

Just look at this place. It has been so neglected. I'm going to fix up this house and get back into my farming. I still think wheat is the crop of the future, so I'll rotate it with another crop and see if I can't become a gentleman farmer. I'll continue to write. After all, I'm not ready to let go of my own convictions. And you, James?

James:

Oh, I'll go right back into the thick of things in Washington. It's in my blood. If I were smart, I'd get out, too, but I just can't let it go. By the way, John Adams asked me to tell you to get in touch with him once you're settled in. He said he misses your engaging conversations.

Thomas:

He was a good friend to me when I was his vice-president. I'll have to write him soon. Time has really created a chasm between me and so many of my friends. I need to get back to what is important in life.

James:

Well, don't forget me as you write. I hope you'll always consider me a friend, even if I did give you bad advice.

Thomas:

You'll always be a dear friend, James. As for your giving me bad advice, you really didn't. You told me what I secretly wanted to hear. You didn't force me into anything, James. I could have walked out at any point. In fact, each time, I did. I just didn't have the good sense to walk out soon enough. But I have learned my lesson. I do know I'll never walk back into the politics of Washington.

Narrator:

For the next 19 years, Jefferson farmed, wrote, and kept in contact with his many friends. By donating his extensive personal library to it after the burning of Washington in the War of 1812, Jefferson helped ensure the continuation of the Library of Congress. He also was a leading force in the establishment of the University of Virginia at Charlottesville. Once the university was founded, he played a major role in all aspects of its early success. He served as rector and as architect of its buildings, he sought to hire the best teachers, and he took an active role in determining what subjects would be taught. At Monticello he used his knowledge of science to incorporate dumbwaiters, a disappearing bed, and unusual lighting and ventilation features into his home's interior. As the years waned, John Adams became Jefferson's closest friend. Ironically, they both died on July 4, 1826.

Secrets at the Mardi Gras*

BACKGROUND INFORMATION

Although these Mardi Gras festivities take place in New Orleans, Louisiana, the holiday was originally celebrated in France. It celebrates Shrove Tuesday, the day before Ash Wednesday, which begins the season of Lent. As in this story, some of the lure of Mardi Gras has to do with the keeping of many secrets, among them the identity of the Mardi Gras royalty and King Rex, who rides in the parade on a float. Mardi Gras highlights include the appearance of the float itself, the anticipation of receiving small gifts, and the discovery of the identities of those people who attend the parade and balls hidden behind great masks until sundown. The following story is the adventure of a young boy who tries to find out one of the secrets of Mardi Gras before everyone else.

STAGING

The narrator for this script should be physically separated from the action. Therefore, you may want the Narrator to sit or stand to the side of the room or in the back. The main staging area will need to represent five locations: outside the den, inside the den, inside a house, in front of the house, and outside on the street where the parade takes place. Chairs could be set in small semicircles to indicate each area; however, this particular script does lend itself to movement more than most. If the class has performed several scripts and is able to manage movement, this is a good script to use.

Though time constraints will dictate the elaborateness of production of this script, it lends itself well to the use of fancy masks, which the students could create during art class. Students should be encouraged to bring in items from home to use on the masks: feathers, buttons, bits of old jewelry, or loose "gemstones." Pasta in various shapes could also be painted and used as decorative items. Four of the masks need to represent purple goblins. Making masks would help nonreaders feel part of this story, and they could all join in after the staging to form a parade around the room. For older students, floats that they create could become the focal point of an art or a home project. The floats could be stationary or mobile, depending on how they are going to be used in the classroom environment or as part of the parade.

---

*Adapted from Joan Constantino and Josephine Constantino, "Secrets at Mardi Gras," in *Holiday Story Book* (New York: Thomas Y. Crowell, 1952).

The staging also lends itself to the use of creative background scenery painted on cardboard, which provides a good way to manage the scene changes and avoid confusion for the audience. If the class has time to make the backdrops, along with the floats and masks, an organized time frame for managing all of these is strongly suggested. All props should be completed the week before the planned presentation so students can practice using them as they work with their scripts.

The Mardi Gras script begins outside with the boys playing. The action then moves to the outside of the dens and then inside one of the dens. Next, the action will move inside Victor's house, then outside in front of it, and, finally, out onto the street for the parade.

CHARACTERS

Narrator, Victor, Émile, Jacques, Papa Rolland, Mother, two young boys (who will be goblins with Victor and Émile), and other parade watchers or participants as the teacher sees fit.

Secrets at the Mardi Gras

Narrator:

It is the Wednesday evening before Shrove Tuesday in New Orleans. Victor's father, Papa Rolland, and other carpenters have been working hard as they build the Mardi Gras parade floats. The work, which began last spring, has been done during the evenings. The floats are build inside warehouses along the river. These warehouses are called dens. No one is allowed to see the floats except the workers. Because the floats are hidden from view, their appearance always causes a great deal of interest. Because Victor Rolland's father works on the floats, his friends envy him. However, he has never been allowed inside the dens. Victor and his friend, Émile, are walking toward one of the dens with Papa Rolland's supper.

Victor:

Tomorrow is the day, Émile! We will get to dress in our costumes and go to the parade.

Émile:

What does the big float look like this year?

Victor:

I don't know. You know it is a surprise.

Émile:

Well, you should know what it looks like. Your father works on it every day. Hasn't he told you?

Victor:

Of course not! Everybody knows the big float must be kept secret until the day of the Mardi Gras. My father would never betray a trust.

Émile:

I dare you to go into the den and find out what the float looks like. If you do, I will buy you four snowballs.

Victor:

Émile, no one is allowed in the dens but the carpenters.

Émile:

I know that, but if anyone can do it, you can. I have the money right here in my pocket for four snowballs. You know how much you like them, Victor. What do you say?

Narrator:
Victor wondered how he could get into the den. He did love snowballs. The thought of the shaved ice balls dipped into sweet syrup—four of them all to himself!—was too much of a temptation.

Victor:
All right, I'll do it.

Émile:
I'll want proof. When I see the proof, then you'll get the ices. How are you going to get in?

Victor:
I don't know, yet. But I'll find a way, and when I do, I will bring you a small piece of the float for proof. You be careful what you say around Jacques, hear me?

Émile:
Sure, I don't want to give you away.

Victor:
Good evening, Jacques.

Jacques:
Bonsoir, good evening. I see you have your papa's supper. Are you excited about tomorrow, boys?

Victor:
Oh, yes we are. We were wondering if we could take a peek at the float tonight. After all, the parade is tomorrow.

Jacques:
Oh, no! No one may see the float before the parade. You know that, Victor.

Émile:
Why not? Why is this such a big secret?

Jacques:
The secrets of Mardi Gras have been passed down in our families since our grandfathers came here from France. The Mardi Gras celebration is our custom on the feast day of Shrove Tuesday, or Fat Tuesday. It reminds us of the French peasants who would lead a fat ox through the village streets so people would remember that it was the last day they could eat meat until Easter. The floats are like the ox, and it is their secrets that make the carnival exciting.

Victor:
Did they celebrate with a carnival in France as big as ours?

Jacques:
No! Only in New Orleans is there a celebration as magnificent as ours.

Papa Rolland:
And this year will be more magnificent than ever! I see you have my supper, Son.

Victor:
Yes, Papa.

Papa Rolland:
Thank you for bringing it. Now, you two run along home. Jacques, we are ready for the barrels.

Jacques:
All right, Rolland. I will begin to carry them in.

Victor:
Jacques, what are the barrels for?

Jacques:
They are the seats on the float. They will be decorated so beautifully that even you will not know the seats are old barrels. You go along now. I have a lot of work to do to get all of these barrels inside.

Victor:
Émile, let's go home now. Come on. I have a lot to do tonight, don't you?

Émile:
Yes, but I . . .

Victor:
Shh! I don't want Jacques to hear my plan. Let's go hide around the corner. Come on.

Émile:
What is your plan?

Victor:

We will watch for Jacques to take the next barrel into the den. Then, we will race to the barrels and I will get into one. You need to put the top on and then run out of sight so Jacques does not see you. Then, Jacques will carry me into the den. When everyone leaves, I will get out of the barrel. Not only will I see the float, but you will owe me four snowballs. Will you help me?

Émile:

Oh, yes, Victor! What a great plan. I knew you would come up with something. But remember, you promised to bring me a piece of the float.

Victor:

I will. Hurry, there goes Jacques back into the den.

Narrator:

Once inside the dark, small, cramped barrel, Victor was carried into the den by Jacques. Victor was afraid to breathe too deeply for fear the barrel would fall apart. It was very warm inside the den, and before long, Victor had fallen asleep. Finally, all of the noise stopped, the lights went out, and the workers went home to get ready for the next day. The quiet woke Victor up. He carefully pushed the top of the barrel up, and the only light in the room came from the moon as it shone through the windows of the den. Victor carefully climbed out of the barrel. He could not believe his eyes. There was the big float. It looked like a giant wedding cake. The float was covered with tinsel and flowers. It was the biggest and most beautiful float Victor had ever seen. This was the float of Rex, King of the Carnival. From the border of silver leaves, Victor took one leaf to show Émile. Then, quickly, Victor ran home. The next morning, Victor woke to the sound of pebbles being thrown against his bedroom window.

Émile:

Hurry up and get dressed, Victor.

Victor:

I'll be right down.

Mother:

Well, look here. Finally our little purple goblin has decided to get up. When I answered the door a few minutes ago, there were three other goblins all dressed in bright Mardi Gras costumes. I don't suppose you know who they are, do you?

Victor:

Mother, you know I don't! How could I know who is behind those masks?

Papa Rolland:
I'd guess they are friends of yours. They are much too short to be anyone who would come to see me. Why not open the door and let the goblins in, now that you are ready?

Victor:
Okay. Hey, goblins, come on in and let my Papa see if he knows who you are!

Papa Rolland:
My, my! I thought it would be easy to figure out who these goblins are, Mother. I guess I was wrong. Do you know who they are?

Mother:
No, I don't. But one thing is for sure, you are the four best-looking goblins I have ever seen.

Émile:
Thanks, Mrs. Rolland. Well, Victor, are you ready to go?

Victor:
May I leave now? Please?

Papa Rolland:
I guess so. I'll bet the next time I see you four, you will be right in front of the crowds at the parade. Just wait until you see the big float, goblins. It's great!

Victor:
(Whispering to Émile) I've already seen it. I have your proof right here. Let's go so I can show it to you.

Émile:
Good-bye, everyone. We've got lots to see. Let's go.

Other Goblins:
(In chorus) Bye!

Émile:
Come on, Victor. We're outside now. Let me see your proof.

Victor:
Okay. Here is a leaf from the side of the float.

Émile:
It's a beautiful silver leaf, Victor. How do I know it really came from the float?

Victor:
When the float goes by, I will show you where it fits.

Narrator:
The boys dashed off in the direction of Canal Street, where the parade would be. Everywhere they went, there were people dressed in the traditional green, purple, and yellow colors of Mardi Gras. There were carts selling flowers, candy, bags of peanuts and popcorn, bright-colored balloons, and colored dusters. The air was filled with the sounds of the tinkling bells and blowing horns used to mark the celebration. Everyone wore a mask. Some looked like animals, others like clowns or pirates. The sights made Victor feel as if he were walking in a dreamland. A loud cheer came from the crowd on Canal Street as the parade started toward them. Quickly, the four boys formed a chain as they plunged through the crowd to stand in front.

Émile:
Have you ever seen such beautiful sights!

Victor:
Here it comes, Émile. Here comes the float that my leaf is from. See, there are the silver leaves, just like this one.

Émile:
Yes, I see them, Victor. You really did it! You got in to see the float before anyone else saw it. I guess I owe you four snowballs. Let's go find the vendor's cart.

Narrator:
Victor shared his snowballs with his three friends. Victor thought the one he kept for himself was the best snowball he'd ever had. The rest of the day, the boys joined in all of the different celebrations of Mardi Gras. At dusk everyone came back to Canal Street for the final parade. This was a torchlight parade in honor of Comus, the god of festival, joy, and mirth. Thirty men with torches surrounded the golden coach of Comus. Following the coach was a float filled with masked riders. Each rider had a silk bag filled with gifts to be tossed into the crowd.

Émile:
Look at the chains and candy that they are throwing. I wish they'd throw something to me.

Victor:
Me, too. Please, please, throw me something!

Émile:
I don't believe it! That masker called you the purple goblin and threw you that gold chain. You are the luckiest person I know.

Victor:
Why do you say that?

Émile:
Last night you saw the float. Tonight you get a gift. I'd say you're lucky.

Victor:
Maybe so. But one thing I know for sure, Émile: This is the best Mardi Gras I've ever seen!

St. Patrick's Day

A Pinch of Green

BACKGROUND INFORMATION

Like many of our traditional holidays, St. Patrick's Day is religious in origin. It is an Irish celebration of the conversion of the Irish to Christianity by St. Patrick in the 400s. Now widely celebrated in the United States, the holiday is most often associated with its most prominent symbol, the shamrock. The shamrock, with its three leaves, symbolizes the Trinity of the Christian church.

Schoolchildren celebrate the day by wearing green—sometimes a traditional green shamrock, sometimes a green article of clothing. The color is considered lucky because in Irish folklore, the little men found waiting at the end of the rainbow with the pot of gold are wearing green. Many children also enjoy pinching those who fail to wear green (the pinch represents the bad luck incurred by failing to wear the lucky color). Though the pot of gold at the end of the rainbow doesn't exist, the traditional pinch certainly does, and this custom forms the basis of this St. Patrick's Day script. This script would make a good introduction to an art lesson on making shamrocks or shamrock people as part of a March art program.

STAGING

The Narrator should sit or stand to the left of the stage while the other readers stand in the center of the staging area. The teacher will need to walk onstage. Once the teacher has entered, the readers can sit on stools or on the floor of the staging area. You may want to have a green paper shamrock and green paper as props for the end of the skit.

CHARACTERS

Narrator, Cassie, Audrey, Paul, and Teacher.

A Pinch of Green

Narrator:

As our story opens, it is March 17th, Saint Patrick's Day, honoring a priest who built many churches and schools in Ireland a long time ago. Not only does everyone pretend to be Irish on this day, but they all wear green. In some places, if you don't wear green, you get pinched, as Cassie has just found out.

Audrey:

Cassie, don't cry! You're all right. Paul didn't mean to hurt you.

Cassie:

But it did hurt. Why did you pinch me, Paul?

Paul:

You're not wearing any green.

Cassie:

That's no reason to pinch me! *(cries louder)*

Teacher:

My goodness, Cassie, what's the matter?

Audrey:

Paul pinched her.

Teacher:

Paul, did you really pinch Cassie?

Paul:

Yes.

Teacher:

Paul, I'm surprised at you. Why did you pinch her?

Paul:

Because she doesn't have on any green.

Audrey:

Paul says she's supposed to wear green 'cause it's St. Patrick's Day. She didn't, so he pinched her.

Cassie:

And it was a hard pinch, too.

Teacher:
I see. I think you all had better sit down while we talk about this. Paul, why would you pinch someone for not wearing green?

Paul:
I don't know. I just know if you don't wear green, you get pinched.

Teacher:
I see. So if I didn't have on green today, you would have pinched me, too?

Paul:
Well, I don't know. Maybe.

Teacher:
Let's just say you would, okay? What kind of a pinch would it have been, a hard pinch or just a quick little pinch?

Paul:
A quick little pinch. That's what I gave Cassie. I didn't do it very hard.

Cassie:
Yes, you did. You pinched me as hard as you could. It hurt.

Paul:
It wasn't my hardest pinch. I could've pinched harder. You're just a baby.

Cassie:
I am not. You pinched me hard on purpose.

Teacher:
All right, children, that's enough. Paul, while you may have thought it was a quick little pinch, to Cassie it really did hurt. I think you need to understand that this kind of pinching, if you are going to do it, is just in fun and should not hurt anyone. It should hardly be felt. And Cassie, I don't think Paul pinched you quite as hard as you're saying he did. I think you're more upset because you forgot to wear green today. Paul, I know you were just having fun, but I want you to tell Cassie you are sorry you hurt her.

Paul:
Okay. Cassie, I'm sorry it hurt. It was just in fun.

Audrey:
I wish I had something green I could give you, Cassie, so you won't get pinched all day long.

Teacher:

I have an idea. Why don't we make green shamrocks, and Cassie can pin one on her shirt?

Paul:

Yeah, that's a great idea. But what does one look like?

Teacher:

Like this. See, it has a stem and three leaves that come together in the middle on top of the stem.

Narrator:

It wasn't long before Cassie and her friends had made several shamrocks. With the shamrock pinned on her shirt, no one else pinched Cassie the rest of the day, so she had good luck—just like everyone else who wore green!

A Happy Easter*

BACKGROUND INFORMATION

This story is set in Czechoslovakia during the Easter season. The Czech names have been changed to make them easier for students. The story describes the traditions surrounding Easter eggs, which are used to ward off evil spirits and as gifts for friends.

STAGING

The Narrator should sit on a stool at one side of the stage. All other reading takes place center stage. Toward the end of the script, there is some action suggested, which the students can be encouraged to perform if they are comfortable with movement and reading. Baskets of plastic eggs may be used as props, but I discourage any use of sticks for switching.

CHARACTERS

Narrator, Mother, Margaret, Annie, Jack, Marie, Karl, and Edward.

*Adapted from Helene Pelzel, "A Happy Easter," in *The Easter Book of Legends and Stories*, edited by Alice Isabel Hazeltine and Elva Sophronia Smith (New York: Lothrop, Lee, and Shepard, 1947).

A Happy Easter

Narrator:

Margaret and her family are traveling by train to Aunt Josephine's for Easter. Margaret is looking forward to visiting her aunt because she lives on a little farm. Margaret and her family live in an apartment in the city. Margaret is excited about being able to play outside whenever she wants to. When she is home with her family, she can play only in the courtyard of the apartment building or at a public park. Margaret is getting impatient as the trip continues.

Mother:

It seems we have been on the train a long time, doesn't it Margaret?

Margaret:

Yes, I am so eager to get there. This is the first Easter we have ever spent there, isn't it?

Mother:

It is the first time since you were a baby. Are you looking forward to seeing Annie?

Margaret:

Oh, yes! I can hardly wait!

Narrator:

After the family arrived at Aunt Josephine's, they had dinner and then went to bed, as it had been a long day and everyone was tired. The next morning Margaret woke up to find Annie had already gone down to breakfast.

Annie:

Hello, sleepyhead. I'm glad to see you are finally up and dressed. We have so much to do today.

Margaret:

What will we do today, Annie? Tell me.

Annie:

Today is Maundy Thursday. You know it as Green Thursday. Why do you call it Green Thursday?

Margaret:

We go to church and ask forgiveness for our sins. Then we have to do penance for them. When we have finished our penance, we are given a green branch that represents our forgiveness and a new start.

Annie:
Don't you celebrate the establishment of Communion then?

Margaret:
No. Do you?

Annie:
Yes. That's what we celebrate on the Thursday before Easter. We call it Maundy Thursday. There must be many differences in the way we celebrate Easter.

Margaret:
Mother says there are. You must tell me what to do, Annie. I want to celebrate this Easter just like you do.

Annie:
First, you must finish your breakfast. Then we will help with the cleaning.

Narrator:
That morning they helped with the dishes, the dusting, and the shaking of the feather beds to fluff them. That afternoon as they went past the open door of the barn, they saw Jack with a bunch of willow branches.

Margaret:
What will you do with those, Cousin Jack?

Jack:
These are for Pomlazka.

Margaret:
What is Pomlazka?

Jack:
You'll find out soon enough. I made Annie promise not to tell you so it would be a surprise. You will have to wait until Monday to see it and feel it.

Narrator:
Margaret was very curious about Pomlazka, but there was so much to do, she soon forgot about Jack and his willows. By evening Margaret was very tired. She and Annie had polished all of the furniture, filled the fuel box, and gathered the eggs for the next day. She and Annie talked as they got ready for bed.

Annie:
Tomorrow we can rest. We do not have big meals tomorrow because we fast on Good Friday.

Margaret:
Yes, I know that. In the city we fast, too, and we go to church.

Annie:
We will go early to church and then spend the day quietly. Mother doesn't cook much on Good Friday; that is why there was much to be done today.

Margaret:
Good Friday is a sad day, isn't it?

Annie:
Yes, but I always think of the joyous Easter Day that follows. If there had been no Good Friday, there would be no happy Easter.

Narrator:
It seemed to Margaret that Friday was twice as long as any other day. It was very quiet once they came back from church. The only excitement they had was when they were sent to cut off the branches of the pussy-willow bush.

Margaret:
Aren't these beautiful! Why are we cutting them?

Annie:
You will see tomorrow.

Margaret:
You and Jack. You are full of so many secrets. Each day seems to be full of so many surprises. I can hardly wait for tomorrow.

Narrator:
The next morning when Margaret came down to breakfast, she saw a vase of pussy-willows on each corner of the breakfast table. Under the white tablecloth, straw was lightly spread, and in the center of the table was a round loaf of Easter bread. On the top of the loaf, sugary white, was a cross.

Annie:
We fix the table like this for today only. It is our custom.

Margaret:
What a nice surprise! I can't wait for Pomlazka.

Marie:

Pomlazka is quite different, Cousin Margaret. It is like a game, but I think only boys like it. Annie and I don't like it at all. Perhaps you won't like it, either. After breakfast, we will cook eggs and then color them. Annie will design the eggs with paraffin, then we will dip them into dyes. Perhaps you would like to draw with the paraffin, too?

Margaret:

What will we do with all of the eggs we color?

Annie:

Monday we will take some of them to the sick and shut-in. Poor little Edward, in the cottage on the hillside, will be happy to have some. All day he sits in his chair by the window and watches the roadside. He cannot walk much, and he is often left alone while his grandfather is at work.

Margaret:

May I choose the eggs we give to Edward?

Marie:

Yes, indeed. Pick several for him.

Margaret:

What will we do with the rest of them?

Marie:

Some we will eat and others we need for Pomlazka.

Narrator:

Soon the house was decorated and everything was ready for Easter Day. There were little cakes in the shape of lambs, meat of a very young goat, loaves of special bread, and vegetables ready to be cooked. The girls woke up the next morning to the sounds of family members greeting each other with the words "Christ is risen." After breakfast, they went to church. It seemed to Margaret that the whole day was full of quiet gladness. As the day came to an end, Margaret still had Pomlazka to look forward to, along with giving Edward the special eggs. The next morning Annie and Margaret put some of the eggs in a basket for Grandma Novak and got Edward's basket ready.

Margaret:

What will we do with the rest of the eggs?

Annie:

I don't know.

Margaret:

You do not know! Then why do we put them into the baskets?

Narrator:

Just then Jack came running into the house waving a long switch woven with red ribbons. He began to switch Annie on the legs as Annie dodged about the table. To stop Jack from hitting her, she handed him an egg. As each member of the family came into the kitchen, Jack switched them and would get a colored egg from each of them before he would stop.

Jack:

Now you see why Marie wasn't very happy about Pomlazka?

Margaret:

Oh, yes. Now I see that this is fun only for boys!

Jack:

Well, I really don't hurt anyone. It is just that Annie doesn't like giving up her eggs. And if I didn't switch her, she would not have good health all of the next year. It is time to take the eggs to Edward.

Annie:

Come, we must hurry, Margaret.

Narrator:

On their way to Edward's, Annie and Margaret were stopped by several boys with switches. The extra eggs in their baskets were soon given away to the different boys. Finally, the girls were down to their last few eggs, which they had planned to give to Edward, when Karl came at them with a switch. In trying to avoid his switch, Margaret upset her basket, and all but one egg fell onto the ground and broke. Angry, she began to cry.

Karl:

I didn't mean to hurt you.

Margaret:

You didn't hurt me. I wanted to take these eggs to Edward. He can't get eggs like you can. I was saving my most beautiful eggs for him, and you broke all but one of them.

Karl:

I am sorry. Here, take any of my eggs that you want. I do not need all of them. I do this only for fun. Here, take this one, too, as a gift from me to Edward.

Margaret:
Oh, thank you. That is so kind. Why don't you come with us?

Narrator:
The three children walked quickly to Edward's house. They could see him sitting in the window as they walked up the lane.

Edward:
Come in. I was watching you from the window. You seemed to be having such a good time.

Annie:
We came to bring you these eggs. They are from all of us.

Edward:
Thank you for the eggs. They are beautiful! I shall save the purple one to eat last. The others will make a good supper for Grandfather and me.

Narrator:
At the end of their visit, the girls left Karl with Edward. Karl was showing Edward how to make a whistle from the willow branch. When the girls returned home, Margaret's mother asked her how her day had gone.

Margaret:
This has been the very nicest Eastertide I have ever had. I do hope we can come back again next year. Not only have I learned all about Pomlazka, but Edward and Karl have become friends. What Easter gift could be nicer?

April Fool's Day

Who's the Fool?

BACKGROUND INFORMATION

Although the origins of this holiday are uncertain, April Fool's Day can be traced back to France to the year 1564, when the calendar was changed and the first day of the new year was moved from April 1st to January 1st. If you did not make the change in your calendar, you were caught and thus were considered an "April fool." April Fool's Day is always popular with children, who try to fool their peers and adults with harmless pranks such as putting salt in the sugar bowl. It is especially exciting for children when April Fool's falls on a school day, because they have more people to try to fool. However, as children have become more sophisticated, it has been increasingly difficult for children to pull off the pranks. The following story takes place in a school in the 1800s where April Fool's Day was strictly observed.

STAGING

The Narrator should stand to the left of the staging area. Those reading the parts of students should stand facing the audience because the students are outside of the school waiting to get in. The girls should enter the staging area first, then the boys will come along. The teacher should enter from the audience, as if she were in the classroom, behind the locked door. There is some action described in parentheses throughout the dialogue. Actions should be performed if your class has worked on mime. If not, you may want to delete these actions before you print the student copies of the script.

CHARACTERS

Narrator, Linda, Faye, Rob, Marty, and Teacher.

Who's the Fool?

Narrator:

In the 1800s many students went to school in one room. Some one-room schools would have 10 or more students, all of different ages and in different grades, at the same time. One teacher would teach them all. Class members depended on each other for help. If the teacher was busy with one or two students, older students would help the littler ones with their lessons. Usually, the older ones also enjoyed teaching the little ones about April Fool's Day. However, this year two older students are going to get a lesson of their own on April Fool's Day.

Linda:

Why is the door locked?

Faye:

I don't know, but there's the note Miss Pickford said would be on the door.

Linda:

But she didn't say the door would be locked.

Faye:

I wonder where she is? She's always here first. I'm scared. Maybe we should go home and get our parents. Maybe something's gone wrong.

Linda:

Oh, don't be a cry baby. Look, here come Rob and Marty. I'll take the note down and give it to them. They'll tell us what it says.

Rob:

Hey, Linda! Why are your shoes unlaced?

Linda:

(Looking down at shoes) They're not!

Rob:

Caught ya! April Fool!

Linda:

That's not very funny, Rob.

Marty:

Why are you two standing out here? Let's go inside.

Faye:
We can't. The door's locked.

Marty:
Oh, sure it is. You can't fool me. I know it's April 1st. It was a good try, though.

Faye:
Then try to open the door. I bet you can't do it.

Rob:
Come on, Faye. We know you're just trying to trick us. Open the door.

Faye:
I can't. It's locked.

Rob:
Linda, you open it.

Linda:
We told you, it's locked. It really is.

Marty:
Well, Rob, we can't stand here all day. I guess we'll have to play along with them. *(Tries door)* Hey, Rob, it really is locked.

Rob:
I wonder why? Miss Pickford should be here by now. So should all of the other children. I wonder where everyone else is?

Linda:
We told you the door was locked. Here, what does this say?

Rob:
Where was this note, Linda?

Linda:
On the door. What does it say?

Rob:
Marty, look at this note. Do you think this was really on the door?

Marty:
I don't know. I guess it could have been. It looks a little like Miss Pickford's handwriting. Are you sure one of you didn't have someone write this note?

Faye:
No. Anyway, Marty, we can't even read that well yet. What does it say?

Marty:
It says, "Due to the lack of firewood for the potbelly stove, there will be no school today. You may go home until tomorrow. Miss Pickford."

Faye:
Really? We get to go home?

Rob:
I don't know. There's something funny about this.

Marty:
Why do you say that?

Rob:
'Cause last night my dad brought some firewood over in his wagon and set it right here on the porch.

Faye:
Maybe someone stole it?

Linda:
Who would steal firewood from the school?

Faye:
I don't know, but it's gone.

Rob:
That's true, I sure don't see it. I don't know, though. Marty, you're taller than I am. Go look in the window and see if anyone's in there.

Marty:
Oh, come on, Rob. It says no school, so there's no school. Let's just go home.

Rob:
No. Come on, Linda. I'll lift you up on my shoulders, and you can look in the window and see what's going on in there.

Linda:
Okay, just don't drop me.

Rob:
What do you see?

Linda:
Nothing.

Rob:
What do you mean, nothing?

Linda:
Nothing. I don't see anyone or anything.

Rob:
Look over toward the stove. Is there a fire in it?

Linda:
I don't know. The door's closed.

Marty:
Rob, if there was a fire in the stove, you'd see the smoke coming out of the chimney. There's no smoke, no fire, no school. Let's go.

Linda:
Put me down, Rob.

Rob:
Okay. Maybe you're right, Marty. Let's go.

Faye:
Wait. Maybe we ought to knock on the door.

Marty:
Why?

Faye:
Well, if they are in there and they don't know we're out here, why would they open the door?

Linda:
Faye, that's the silliest thing you've said today. How could they not know we're out here? There's no one in there. Let's go home.

Faye:
No, I'm gonna knock first. *(Pretends to knock on door)*

Marty:
See, I told you there's no school, just like the note said. Let's go.

Faye:
I guess you're right. But will you go home with us and tell our parents? I don't think they'll believe us.

Rob:
I guess so. Let's go. *(They start to walk away)*

Teacher:
And where are you four off to? Planning on playing hooky?

Rob:
Miss Pickford! No, we have this note here that says there is no school.

Teacher:
April Fool!

Marty:
You've got to be kidding! Boy, did we get caught, Rob.

Teacher:
We planned this all week. Everyone else got here early, and we've been hiding in the cloakroom waiting for Faye's knock.

Rob:
You mean you two were in on this, too?

Linda:
Well, we knew there was going to be a trick played on you, but Miss Pickford only told Faye and me that when we got here, there would be a note on the door to trick you. Then Faye was to knock just before you did what the note said.

Faye:
But you never said the door would be locked.

Teacher:
No, because if I told you that, I was afraid you'd give it all away. Anyway, if it wasn't locked, they wouldn't have believed the note.

Linda:

I guess so. I was a good April Fool's trick, huh Rob?

Rob:

Yeah, you got us good. Well, Marty, I guess we'd better go inside and get some work done. Looks like our free day isn't so free after all.

Teacher:

Oh, I don't know about that. In honor of April Fool's Day I think we'll only do one subject today and play games the rest of the day.

Marty:

Good try, Miss Pickford. But you won't catch us twice.

Teacher:

In that case, I guess you need to get the fire started in the stove. It's pretty cold inside.

Narrator:

As they joined the other children in the classroom, Miss Pickford did keep her word. They did spend part of the day playing games. But all day long, Rob and Marty wondered when she would say "April Fool!" again.

May Day

From Maypoles to Bees

BACKGROUND INFORMATION

Another spring festival that has lost some of its importance over the years is May Day. It has been celebrated with knots, flowers, May baskets, dancing around the maypole, and even more raucous activities that aren't appropriate for children. However, because of those raucous activities, the Puritans stifled the adult celebrations, and May Day became a lesser holiday. Today, children often make a basket and fill it with flowers or simply put flowers on a neighbor's front porch, ring the bell, and run away so that the neighbor finds only a bouquet of flowers.

In Europe the day is still celebrated with traditional dances around the maypole or bush. Revellers then go door to door with flowers and receive a gift of food in return.

There are many lesser-known beliefs that also go along with May Day. In this script, I will address not only the tradition of presenting flowers to a friend on May Day, but also some of the folklore associated with May 1.

STAGING

The Narrator should stand to the left of the stage. The other readers can sit across the front of the staging area on chairs or stools while they read.

CHARACTERS

Narrator, Janice, Marlene, Marsha, Penny, and Cindy.

From Maypoles to Bees

Narrator:
Tomorrow will be May 1st. The day is traditionally celebrated as the beginning of spring. And there are many different beliefs about the first of May and many different ways of celebrating the beginning of spring.

Janice:
Marlene, tomorrow you should go out before the sun gets up and wash your face with dew.

Marlene:
Why would I want to do that?

Janice:
You're always saying you want to get rid of some of those freckles. If you wash your face with dew and then put your hands somewhere else on your body, the freckles will leave your face and go wherever your hands are.

Marsha:
You can't be serious, Janice.

Janice:
That's what I read in a book about different holidays.

Marsha:
And you believe it'll work?

Janice:
I don't know, but if Marlene tries it, we'll know for sure.

Penny:
Take my advice, Marlene, and forget it. There's no way to get rid of those freckles.

Cindy:
Oh, I don't know about that. My grandmother says if you wash your face in stump water on the first of May, your freckles will go away.

Penny:
Good grief! You guys don't really believe that stuff, do you?

Marlene:
No, but it makes as much sense as rubbing your face with rye three times at sunrise.

Marsha:
Where did you hear that one?

Marlene:
My great-aunt told me that when I was complaining about my freckles. My mother really cracked up over it. I've never seen her laugh so hard in my life. My great-aunt didn't think it was funny. She swears it works!

Penny:
I suppose she saw someone who tried it, and their freckles disappeared?

Marlene:
That's what she says. Even my mother couldn't get her to back off from her story. My great-aunt just got madder the more Mother tried to get her to admit it was just folklore.

Janice:
I guess some people really do believe those things are true. Actually, I was just teasing you.

Marlene:
I know that, but it's interesting the way these things get started. I remember one year my mother wanted to plant watermelon seeds in our garden. My grandmother told her she couldn't plant them until May 1st. If she planted them any other day, they wouldn't come up. On top of that, it had to be done before sun-up.

Cindy:
Did she do it?

Marlene:
No. By the time May 1st came around, she had already planted everything, including watermelon seeds.

Penny:
Did she get any watermelons?

Marlene:
Four or five. We'd have had more, but she fried the watermelon blossoms for dinner one night.

Janice:
Oh, yuck! You didn't eat them did you?

Marlene:
Actually, they were really good.

Cindy:
I suppose there's some old wives' tale about that, too?

Marlene:
I don't know. But Grandma refused to eat them. She said they couldn't be good for you if they were grown from seeds not planted on May 1st. I guess other people believed similar folklore about planting corn.

Janice:
Don't people plant when the ground is ready? Maybe by May 1st the ground is warmer and easier to work. After all, most of the farmers years ago depended on themselves, not machines, to do the work.

Cindy:
You're probably right. The belief I think is really silly is about curing a sore throat. Have any of you heard that one? On May 1st, if you hold someone's mouth up to the sun so a ray of light can enter that person's mouth, the sore throat will go away.

Marsha:
You mean people went all winter with a sore throat waiting for the sun on May 1st? Man, I'd miss half of the school year if I waited for May 1st and sunshine. I wonder what happens if there's no sunshine at all?

Cindy:
I guess you'd have your sore throat until the next May!

Penny:
That's really weird. I wonder how all of these crazy beliefs got started?

Janice:
I don't know, but why don't we celebrate May Day like people used to?

Marlene:
I never knew we celebrated May Day. What did people do?

Janice:
Long ago, they would have a pole with strips of paper or cloth hung from the top. Then children would take hold of the strips and dance around the pole until all of the pole was wrapped.

Cindy:
Can you see the boys in our class dancing around a pole? Why did they do that, anyway?

Janice:
It was just a way to celebrate the beginning of spring. Now we don't do anything.

Penny:
I remember when I lived in Kewanee the little girls next door brought over a bunch of flowers to my mom. They rang the door bell, but when she went to answer it, there were only flowers; no one was around. She had to ask a neighbor about it because she'd never had that happen before.

Cindy:
What did the neighbor tell her?

Penny:
She said that in Kewanee, on the first day of May, kids always bring flowers to the neighbors to celebrate the first day of spring.

Marsha:
That's really neat! No one's ever done that for my mom.

Marlene:
Or mine! Let's do that tomorrow for each other's moms!

Janice:
Hey, yeah! That could be a lot of fun. Why don't we put our moms' names in a hat. We can each pull out a name and give flowers to that person.

Cindy:
Great idea! Where will we get the flowers?

Marlene:
We could make them from tissue paper. That way they would have them for a long time.

Penny:
I'll run home and get my glue and some things to use and be right back.

Marlene:
Me, too. Celebrating May Day with flowers makes a lot more sense than trying to wash off freckles.

Cindy:
Or trying to cure your sore throat, huh Marsha?

Marsha:

Really. Hurry up, you guys, if you're going to go get stuff. I'll get my things ready while you're gone. But remember to be quiet about what we're doing. We don't want to spoil the surprise.

Narrator:

The rest of that afternoon, the girls worked together to make flowers to share with the mothers the next morning. Very early, before they had to leave for school, the girls slipped out of their houses and put the flowers on a mother's porch. They rang the doorbell, then ran and hid as they waited for the door to open. Each mother was surprised to find a newspaper filled with different colored tissue-paper flowers and a note that said, "Happy May Day."

Cinco de Mayo

The Grand Fiesta

BACKGROUND INFORMATION

The Grand Fiesta is in honor of the Mexican holiday Cinco de Mayo, which means the fifth of May. On May 5, 1862, General Ignario Zaragoza led a ragged Mexican army into battle to fight 6,000 well-trained French invaders. As evening fell, more than 1,000 French soldiers had died and the Mexican army had won an important battle that eventually led to the end of the European invasion. Yearly on the fifth of May, Mexican-Americans celebrate this great victory of the Mexican army. Celebrations are held in schools, parks, and homes in Mexican-American communities throughout the country. There is a mixture of music, games, and feasting in honor of Cinco de Mayo. In this script, an American family is traveling in southern California and happens upon a Cinco de Mayo celebration.

STAGING

The Narrator should stand on the left of the staging area with the rest of the readers sitting as if they are in a car. The parents should be sitting on two chairs that are separated enough so that the children in the back two chairs can be seen from the audience.

CHARACTERS

Narrator, Julie, Mother, Dad, and Angie.

The Grand Fiesta

Narrator:

It is May 5th and the Johnson family is traveling in southern California. They have come to a park where a Cinco de Mayo celebration is in progress. General Ignario Zaragoza is being remembered for his part in a battle in Mexico with the French soldiers on May 5, 1862. Cinco de Mayo, which means fifth of May, is a fiesta celebrated by Mexican-Americans in remembrance of this great victory. As the Johnsons arrive at the park, they find a fiesta is underway.

Julie:

Mother, look at all of the people in the park. It looks like a big party.

Mother:

It is a party, only here they call it a fiesta. It's May 5th and they're having a special fiesta in honor of General Ignario Zaragoza, according to my guidebook.

Julie:

Look at all of the dancers in those beautiful costumes. I've never seen such gorgeous dresses. Look at all of those ruffles and such big skirts. What holds them out like that?

Mother:

Crenlans. I used to wear them when I was growing up. But I never had a dress as pretty as those are. These are the dancers. They'll do different dances of their ancestors in Mexico.

Dad:

I am not sure I understand this celebration. What is so important about General Zaragoza?

Mother:

He led the Mexican army against 6,000 French invaders. They fought on May 5th, 1862. The Mexicans only had two small forts in Puebla, Mexico, for protection. From these two forts they fought off the French soldiers and at the end of the day there were over 1,000 French soldiers killed. The Mexicans had defeated the French army. It was a great victory for the Mexican army.

Julie:

Why did the French attack the Mexicans?

Mother:

The French invaded the country to try to take control of it. The Mexicans proved that an army of untrained men, who were determined to retain their freedom, could beat a well-trained and outfitted army.

Angie:
It sounds like the battle was very short.

Mother:
It was, but it was a very important victory. After the French left Mexico, no European country tried to invade North America again.

Angie:
Why doesn't everyone celebrate this day? It seems to me the Mexicans did us a real favor.

Dad:
You're right about that, Angie. Does your book explain why only Mexican-Americans celebrate Cinco de Mayo?

Mother:
No, it just says it is celebrated in many Mexican-American communities. In Mexico Cinco de Mayo is a national holiday.

Julie:
What do you mean by national holiday?

Mother:
That means everyone has the day off to celebrate just like we do Veterans' Day or Thanksgiving.

Angie:
Look at all the brightly colored booths and the dancers and musicians.

Dad:
I know what the musicians are called. They're Mariachi bands. The music is exciting. It makes you want to get up and dance along, doesn't it?

Julie:
Dad, I don't think you could keep up with the dancers that are on that stage. They're moving so fast they make me dizzy just watching them.

Mother:
I think Julie's right about that, dear. Do you want to get out of the car and see what's going on?

Angie:
Sure! Does your book tell us what to expect as we go around the park?

Mother:

Let's see. Hmm, there should be booths where people display things, games to play, food, music, dancers, and this looks interesting. They have digs for archaeological treasures. Then at the end of the day they hang clay piñatas for the children to break. The piñatas are filled with candy.

Julie:

We did that once at school, break a piñata. It was full of candy and little toys. But the one at school was made of paper, not clay. It was hard to break. Everyone had two turns before it broke.

Dad:

Well, come on guys. Let's go. I want to see what games there are and what they have to eat.

Mother:

Good idea. I want to watch the dancers. What do you two want to do?

Julie:

I think I'll go with you. I can't believe how fast they move!

Angie:

Well, I want to play some games, so can I go with you, Dad?

Dad:

Fine with me. Let's see. It's 11:00 o'clock. What if we all meet back here at 1:00 and then we'll see what they have to eat?

Mother:

That's fine with us. Let's go Julie.

Narrator:

The rest of the day the Johnsons joined in the fun of Cinco de Mayo. They watched taco-eating contests, played games, and ate tortillas, while they listened to the Mariachi bands play all day. It was a day where they also made new friends and learned that Cinco de Mayo, whether it is celebrated in the states or Mexico, is a fiesta honoring a great general and an army that fought to keep their country free.

Memorial Day

Remembering

BACKGROUND INFORMATION

Declaration Day, or Memorial Day, is celebrated on the last Monday in May. Although few people may attend the many parades held in honor of our servicemen and -women, this weekend is annually set aside for that purpose. This script focuses on the reasons for celebrating Memorial Day and also makes the students aware that many do not honor the people in our armed services on this day.

STAGING

The Narrator should sit to one side of the staging area. The other three readers should sit center stage, with Grandmother in the middle. A small box with a picture or two inside is the only prop necessary.

CHARACTERS

Narrator, Marnie, Grandmother, and Allyson.

Remembering

Narrator:

Marnie and Allyson are spending a few days with their grandmother. Marnie has found a box of old photographs, and she and Allyson have been spending the afternoon asking Grandmother about them.

Marnie:

Grandma, who is this in the parade?

Grandmother:

That's your grandfather, Marnie.

Marnie:

What kind of a parade was it?

Grandmother:

It was a Declaration Day parade. My, but didn't he look young there?

Allyson:

What is he wearing?

Grandmother:

That was his army uniform.

Allyson:

It must have been a long time ago.

Grandmother:

Yes, it was, Allyson. More than 45 years ago next week.

Marnie:

Why was Grandfather in a parade?

Grandmother:

Well, it was Declaration Day, and he'd just come home after being overseas. In fact, many of the soldiers in this picture came back when he did that August. They were home on a 30-day leave.

Marnie:

What's a leave?

Grandmother:
It's like a vacation. After you have been in the army for so many months, you can take a leave. Well, these men had all been overseas for a long time, so when they got their leave, they all came home to see their families. When leave was over, most of them went back to the army base to finish out their term of service. Once their term was over, many of them came home to stay.

Allyson:
So why was he in the parade?

Grandmother:
There is always a parade on Declaration Day to help people remember those soldiers who died, were wounded, or became living heroes from a war. A lot of soldiers march in these parades every year. This was the first Declaration Day parade after your grandfather had come back from overseas.

Allyson:
You mean Grandfather was in a war? Did he have to shoot people?

Grandmother:
No, he was one of the lucky ones, Allyson. By the time he went overseas, the fighting was over. His job was to help clean up and keep peace. When he came home on leave and Declaration Day came, all of the soldiers got together and went down to march in the parade. They wanted to remember those people who were in the war and show their support for other soldiers who would have to fight in the future.

Marnie:
Was that all they did on Declaration Day?

Grandmother:
No. The parade went through downtown and out to the cemetery. There, people made speeches about the heroes, and there was a 21-gun salute in honor of the dead soldiers.

Marnie:
Did Grandfather shoot his gun?

Grandmother:
No. A special group of soldiers with rifles fires the salute. Why did you think he would shoot a gun?

Marnie:
Because he's wearing a gun in the picture.

Grandmother:
So he is. I didn't notice that. The gun he's wearing in the picture isn't loaded. It's purpose here is more symbolic. As I said, the rifles were shot by a special group of soldiers. They go to funerals and many other events to give this special salute in honor of our servicemen and servicewomen.

Allyson:
Why don't we have Declaration Day anymore, Grandmother?

Grandmother:
Why, we still celebrate it, Allyson. The name has just been changed to Memorial Day. It's always the last Monday of May.

Marnie:
Do we still have parades and go to the cemetery?

Grandmother:
Sure. It isn't a very big parade, but the town still has it.

Allyson:
Do you ever go watch it?

Grandmother:
No, I don't. Your grandfather quit marching in the parades after a few years, and I guess I've just been too busy to go since he died. Haven't you two ever been to a Declaration Day parade?

Marnie:
No. Could we all go to the one next week?

Grandmother:
Of course we can. It's not a very fancy parade. They won't have lots of floats or bands. But it's a very important parade.

Allyson:
Can we go to the cemetery, too?

Grandmother:
Sure! That's the best part. You'll get to hear stories about the bravest people who ever lived.

Marnie:
Will we get to hear the 21-gun salute?

Grandmother:
Yes, and if you're really lucky, when the rifles eject the shell casings, you may even be able to get a casing.

Marnie:
Can I keep it?

Grandmother:
You sure can. In fact, if I look in your grandfather's things, I bet I can find the shell casing he saved from that first parade day.

Allyson:
Grandma, have there been a lot of wars?

Grandmother:
Yes, Allyson, there have been. Some were very short, and some were very long. But in each war, men and women were killed or injured. It's these people that we want to remember. If it hadn't been for them, we wouldn't be living in such a great country. I'm glad we spent the afternoon looking at these old photographs. It's been a good reminder of my past. And thanks to you, we will all get to spend a day together remembering all of the soldiers and the deeds they have done. It's a wonderful holiday, and everyone should remember why we have it.

Marnie:
I can hardly wait, can you, Allyson?

Allyson:
No. It'll be a great day, I just know it.

Flag Day

The Defense of Fort McHenry

BACKGROUND INFORMATION

Very little is made of the War of 1812, the second war between the former colonies and England. Once again, the Americans fought on their own soil, but they were more aggressive in this war and took the fight into Canada as well. It was believed they could take the British stronghold in Canada and force Britain to retreat from North America. They were unsuccessful, and the war dragged on into 1814. It was in September of that year that Francis Scott Key and John S. Skinner attempted to rescue their friend William Beanes from the British prisoner-of-war boat that was anchored in Chesapeake Bay. It was during this event in history that Key wrote "The Defense of Fort McHenry." The first stanza was later set to music and adopted as the "Star-Spangled Banner." Students will not only find the war interesting but may be quite surprised to find that the "Star-Spangled Banner" comes from a much longer poem and, more surprisingly, that it is sung to the melody of an old English drinking song. Finding other well-known lyrics sung to old drinking melodies could make an interesting research project for the students.

STAGING

The Narrator should stand or sit center stage. The readers in the opening scene should stand to the Narrator's left. As the action moves to the boat, Francis should walk behind the Narrator and join the readers on the Narrator's right for the second scene. Readers should also move behind the Narrator to take their places for the third scene. Because there will be more people on the Narrator's left in the third scene than the first scene, it would be a good idea to have enough seats for the third scene already in place when the first scene opens. Those people who do not have to move may remain seated at all times to avoid entering and exiting the staging area. The only necessary prop is a letter with prewritten stanzas on it for Abbie to read from at the end of the script.

CHARACTERS

Narrator, Abbie, Francis, Sailor, Captain, John, Mr. Smith, and William.

The Defense of Fort McHenry

Narrator:

It was September 13, 1814. For the last two years, the United States had been at war with England. This was the War of 1812, and it was being fought in both the United States and Canada over trading rights. The Americans attacked the British stronghold in Canada, hoping to bring it down. Unfortunately for the Americans, this proved impossible. Meanwhile, during a battle on the East Coast, William Beanes, a doctor who had ordered the imprisonment of three British stragglers, was taken prisoner by the British. He was being held in a British prisoner-of-war boat in the Chesapeake Bay at Baltimore, Maryland. His friends, Francis Scott Key and John S. Skinner, received special permission to approach the captain of the boat and ask for William's release.

Abbie:

Francis, I've been told that you and John are going to go to the bay and try to talk the British captain into letting William off of the prisoners' boat. Are you crazy? They aren't going to listen to you. You'll only put yourselves in jeopardy.

Francis:

Abbie, I understand your concern, but we have to get William off of that boat. As bad as his health is, he cannot stay on that boat long without proper care. We must see if we can convince the British to let him go.

Abbie:

And if they won't let him go, what are you prepared to do?

Francis:

We'll figure that out when the time comes.

Abbie:

Good luck! I'm anxious to hear how this goes. Come by my house afterward and let me know. I don't have a good feeling about this, Francis.

Francis:

You fret too much. Trust me. We'll all be back here by sundown.

Abbie:

I hope you're right.

Narrator:

As Francis and John rowed their dinghy out to the British boat, Francis's earlier words of conviction no longer rang true. He was beginning to wonder if Abbie was right. Maybe he really was crazy. Here he was in a small dinghy, rowing around warships toward the enemy. As he and John neared the prisoners' boat, they heard a sailor yell to the captain.

Sailor:

Captain, there's a small dinghy heading this way. Should we shoot?

Captain:

Who's aboard? Do they look armed?

Sailor:

There are two men, Sir. They don't appear to be armed. In fact, one just started waving a white flag.

Captain:

Then let them approach but watch them carefully. It could be a trick.

Sailor:

Yes, Sir.

Narrator:

As Francis pulled the dinghy alongside the British boat, he announced their desire to come aboard and speak with the captain. Once they had been allowed to board, the captain greeted them on the main deck.

Captain:

Well, gentlemen. Whom do we have here?

Francis:

Francis Scott Key and John S. Skinner.

Captain:

What is so important that you have risked your lives to row out to our boat?

Francis:

We believe you have a friend of ours on board. We would like to talk to you about him. His name is William Beanes.

Captain:

Could be. What's it to you if we do?

Francis:
Mr. Beanes is not a well man. We came to plead with you to let him leave with us. He is in need of constant medical care.

Captain:
You cannot be serious, Mr. Key! You expect me to let you remove one of my prisoners because he is sick! If I were to let all of the sick prisoners on this boat leave, I'd have an empty ship. I can assure you my superiors would frown on that, Mr. Key.

John:
We're not asking you to let all prisoners who are, or may become, sick leave. We are asking only for Mr. Beanes's release as he is in such ill health already.

Captain:
And what do I get in exchange, pray tell?

Francis:
Me.

Captain:
I beg your pardon? Are you telling me you are willing to exchange yourself for this Beanes? You can't be serious!

Francis:
Yes, I am. If you'll let John row William back to shore, I shall stay on the ship in his place.

Captain:
Hmm! Mr. Key, I think you may be crazier than all of the British and Americans who thought this war was necessary. I'll consider your request. However, for now you will both stay on board this boat. Obviously, Mr. Beanes is very important to you, but I am not prepared to let anyone off of this boat just yet. Mr. Smith!

Mr. Smith:
Yes, Captain?

Captain:
Go below and find this William Beanes. Bring him up on deck so he can see his friends.

Narrator:

Although the captain never fully understood Francis's reasoning in offering to exchange himself for William Beanes, he was impressed that these men felt so strongly about a friend. Fully intending to let all three of the men leave, the captain nevertheless decided to hold them on the boat until the next morning. There was to be a major attack on Fort McHenry that night. Knowing the sailors talked freely around the prisoners, the captain was not sure what William knew about the British military plans. That evening while sitting on deck, Francis watched as the British attacked Fort McHenry. The attack was so massive that Francis was sure the fort would be gone in the morning. However, as the sun rose and the mist cleared, Francis saw the U.S. flag still flying over the fort. His pride in his flag and his country was so strong that he began to write a poem.

Later that day, on September 14, 1814, Francis, John, and William were released from the prisoner-of-war boat. They returned home to find Abbie anxiously awaiting their arrival.

Francis:

What are you doing down here on the docks, Abbie? Don't you realize how dangerous it is?

Abbie:

When you didn't return last evening, I became very concerned. No one seemed to know what had happened to you. Then the fort was attacked. I was sure I would never see any of you again. I came down here to ask whether anyone had heard anything today.

William:

Francis and John, I cannot thank you two enough for obtaining my release from that wretched place. I was sure I would die in that boat's hold. But I understand Abbie's concern. You took an awful risk for me.

Abbie:

I guess by now, William, we should know these two well enough to realize that they wouldn't let you die out there, regardless of the cost to themselves. How did the three of you spend your evening?

John:

In all of that commotion, and as we watched in horror as the fort was being attacked, Francis began writing poetry!

Abbie:

You did? What could you possibly write about under those conditions?

Francis:

Actually, I didn't start writing until this morning. We were on deck at sunrise, and lo and behold, there was the flag, still flying over the fort. I was so thrilled that next thing I knew, I had pulled an old letter out of my breast pocket and started writing. The poem is not quite finished yet, but if you'd like to read what I have written, here it is.

William:

Read it out loud, Abbie. We'd all like to hear what Francis wrote.

Abbie:

"Oh! say, can you see, by the dawn's early light,
What so proudly we hailed at the twilight's last gleaming?
Whose broad stripes and bright stars, thro' the perilous fight,
O'er the ramparts we watched were so gallantly streaming?
And the rockets' red glare, the bombs bursting in air,
Gave proof thro the night that our flag was still there.
Oh! say, does that star-spangled banner yet wave
O'er the land of the free and the home of the brave!

On the shore, dimly seen thro' the mist of the deep,
Where the foe's haughty host in dread silence reposes,
What is that which the breeze, o'er the towering steep,
As it fitfully blows, half conceals, half discloses?
Now it catches the gleam of the morning's first beam,
In full glory reflected, now shines on the stream.
'Tis the star-spangled banner. Oh! long may it wave
O'er the land of the free and the home of the brave!

And where is that band who so vauntingly swore
That the havoc of war and the battle's confusion . . . "

Francis, it's wonderful!

Francis:

Thank you, Abbie. I need to finish it. In fact, I think, after hearing you read it, I shall go directly home and do that. I shall bring it by when it is completed.

Abbie:

I look forward to reading it, Francis.

Narrator:

Francis finished his poem that afternoon. By the next day you could find copies of it all over the area. It was printed by a local printer on handbills and given to everyone who walked down the city streets. Within just a few days, the poem was sung in a local tavern to the tune of an old English drinking song. In March 1931, the U.S. Congress officially approved the song as our national anthem. Although we sing only the first stanza, the poem does have four altogether. It was completed as follows:

"And where is that band who so vauntingly swore
That the havoc of war and the battle's confusion
A home and a country should leave us no more?
Their blood has washed out their foul footstep's pollution.
No refuge could save the hireling and slave
From the terror of flight or the gloom of the grave,
And the star-spangled banner in triumph doth wave
O'er the land of the free and the home of the brave.

Oh! thus be it ever when freemen shall stand
Between their loved home and the war's desolation,
Blest with vict'ry and peace, may the Heav'n-rescued land
Praise the pow'r that hath made and preserved us a nation.
Then conquer we must, when our cause it is just,
And this be our motto—'In God is our trust.'
And the star-spangled banner in triumph shall wave
O'er the land of the free and the home of the brave."

The Newbedford Fourth of July

BACKGROUND INFORMATION

The United States celebrates its birthday, Independence Day, on the Fourth of July. Many celebrate the holiday without giving much thought to the reason for the celebration. In this script, one family discusses the planning of their town's first Fourth of July celebration. The script is intended to show students how much work goes into these celebrations as well as the reason for the celebration.

STAGING

The Narrator should stand on the left of the staging area. The other readers should sit in a semicircle as if they are around a table. If you wish, put a table on the staging area and use props to represent breakfast.

CHARACTERS

Narrator, Martha, Thomas, Sara, and Judith.

The Newbedford Fourth of July

Narrator:

It is January 1784 in Newbedford and the city council recently met to begin planning the town's first Independence Day celebration. Independence Day is celebrated on July 4th, the anniversary of the day the Declaration of Independence was signed. The holiday was instituted to celebrate the freedom of the United States from the rule of the British. With the celebration just six months away it was time to determine what events would take place and who would be responsible for these events. Thomas, a member of the city council, and his wife, Martha, are sitting down to breakfast with their children, Sara and Judith. Martha asks Thomas about the meeting.

Martha:

Thomas, you were very late last evening. What took so long?

Thomas:

Jeremiah decided it was time to start planning this year's Independence Day celebration. It took the council 15 minutes just to decide he was right. Then it took another hour and a half to decide what was going to happen and who was going to be in charge of the different events.

Martha:

What are you in charge of?

Thomas:

Mine is easy. I am in charge of getting music for the parade and for the park.

Sara:

Parade! When is there going to be a parade?

Thomas:

Next July 4th.

Sara:

Not until then? That's so far away.

Judith:

Why is there going to be a parade on July 4th, Daddy?

Thomas:

It's a celebration. Actually, I guess you could say it's a birthday party. It will be one year from the day that we declared our complete independence from British rule of our country. Every city is going to plan some kind of celebration, and we're going to start ours with a parade.

Martha:
Hopefully you plan to have more than just music in this parade.

Thomas:
Oh, yes. Ed Campbell is in charge of the groups who will march in the parade, like the soldiers and church groups.

Sara:
Why do you need music at the park?

Thomas:
There is going to be a big party there. Everyone is going to go to the park after the parade to play games, eat food, and then watch fireworks.

Martha:
It sounds like the council planned a pretty interesting day.

Judith:
What kind of games will there be?

Thomas:
I don't know. Perhaps you can ask Mr. Elmore. He's in charge of the games and is to ask your teacher for help in planning them. In fact, maybe you could help him. Why not ask your friends what kind of games they'd like to play and then tell him. He can select the ones he thinks are best, and then he'd know how many prizes to get.

Sara:
Can I help you, Judith? I love to play games.

Judith:
Sure! That's a great idea, Daddy. I know we can come up with a great list of games. Do we have to have all the rules for him?

Martha:
I am sure he'd like them. After all, he's probably never heard of or played some of the games you play, and a list of rules would make it much easier for him. Thomas, who's in charge of food?

Thomas:
Boy, was that a sore spot last night. Everyone argued that for the longest time. Some people thought everyone should have to bring their own. Others thought that wasn't fair because some of the women would be busy with games or in the parade and wouldn't have time to cook. It was a mess.

Martha:
So how did you finally resolve it?

Thomas:
Ted suggested asking the different churches to do food booths. So he became chairman of that! I don't think he was very happy, but it was his idea and a good one at that. He'll have some time trying to decide which church should get to do which booth. I know he's planning on six different ones already.

Martha:
What if you don't want to buy food from a booth?

Thomas:
Oh, you can pack food to take. But this day is planned to end around 9 o'clock at night so I don't think anyone will want to pack that much food.

Judith:
Why will it end so late?

Thomas:
As soon as it's dark they are going to have a fireworks show while the band plays.

Sara:
I don't like fireworks. They make so much noise.

Martha:
That's true, they do. But the noise is a reminder of the cannons and gunfire from the war. If it weren't for those noises we wouldn't be celebrating anything.

Judith:
Was that war really necessary? Some of my friends lost fathers and grandfathers in that war.

Martha:
Yes, it was Judith. If there had not been a war, then we would still be ruled by the British government.

Sara:
Was that so bad?

Thomas:

Yes it was. You see, all the laws we lived under were made in England, and we didn't have any say on many things that affected us. The British Parliament raised our taxes to tremendous levels and we couldn't do a thing about it. They also wouldn't allow us to do business with other countries. Everything we bought had to be purchased through Britain.

Judith:

Don't we still get things from Britain?

Martha:

Yes, we do, but now we can control how much we are willing to pay the British to send it to us. That way if they don't want to sell it to us at our price, we can ask another country to sell it to us.

Judith:

I can see why we'd get a better deal for what we want that way. We can choose who we want to buy things from and get the best price.

Thomas:

Exactly. It has made trading much more profitable for our country. Also, without British rule, we can make our own decisions about laws and how to run our country. It's just a better way to deal with things. Sometimes we'd have to wait months to make a decision because we'd have to send a letter of request to England by ship and then wait for the answer to return by another ship. It was a slow, awkward process. This way things can be done much faster. It makes our government run more smoothly.

Sara:

Do all of the fireworks have to be noisy?

Martha:

Sara, that's what fireworks are.

Thomas:

Actually, Martha, Stimme suggested we spend some money on some of the showy ones. There are some that make just a little noise and are really pretty. They cost a lot more, however. But we decided to buy a few of those, too. They'll be the last ones used, Sara, so you can keep your ears covered until you see the big pretty ones in the sky.

Judith:

When you started talking about a celebration that was seven months away, I didn't understand why you'd plan it now. But it sounds like it's a lot of work to plan a day like this. Are you sure you started soon enough?

Thomas:

I don't know. Since this is our first Fourth of July no one knows the answer to that until it's over. On July 5th we'll know if we started planning soon enough and if we remembered to plan for everything and everyone. I am sure we have forgotten some things. But that's okay. That just means that next year's Fourth of July will be even better.

Martha:

Before you plan for next year, I think you have your hands full planning the music for this year. When do you intend to start lining up groups?

Thomas:

As soon as I get to the office, and I'm late already. You three have a good day. I'll see you after 4 o'clock. Bye.

Narrator:

As you can see, the first Fourth of July in Newbedford was well planned. Today's celebrations are also planned far in advance. In fact, in some cities the committees begin planning for the following year's parade on the fifth of July. They work very hard to make each year's parade different and exciting, as do all other committees who work to make the Fourth of July a special celebration.

Labor Day

The Parade of Surprises

BACKGROUND INFORMATION

This script, based on fact, is the story of the first Labor Day parade, September 5, 1882.

STAGING

The Narrator should remain in the performance area, slightly off to one side and back. The shop should be positioned close to the Narrator, allowing room for the parade to pass by. The rally should take place on the side of the stage opposite the Narrator. Props should include signs for the marchers to carry (the signs should bear the slogans indicated in the script's dialogue).

CHARACTERS

Narrator, Clarice, Father, Mr. McCabe, and three or four Marchers (number may vary if others join the parade as it progresses through the story).

The Parade of Surprises

Narrator:

It is very early on September 5, 1882, when Clarice and her father go to open their shop on Main Street. There has been a lot of talk during the last few weeks about a parade, and Clarice wants to be where she can see everything. Her mother has stayed home with the baby because she and Clarice's father are sure there will be no parade. They believe it is all talk because no one seems to be organizing a parade.

Clarice:

Father, when will the parade begin?

Father:

Clarice, I've told you there may not be any parade today. If it does begin, it will be at 10:30. That's another hour from now. Come away from that window and make yourself useful.

Clarice:

But Father, I don't want to miss anything!

Father:

Clarice, I doubt that you will miss a thing. Now come help me unload these boxes.

Clarice:

Oh, all right. But as soon as I hear anything, I am going back to the window.

Father:

Fine, Clarice. Just come and help me while you wait.

Narrator:

While Clarice and her father continued their work, several streets over, a small group of men and women were lining up for their parade. There were not very many of them, and they were all a little disappointed that so few workers showed up for this parade. Some of the people had signs they had made; others were just going to walk along to show support for the people. Mr. William McCabe was their grand marshal. He was going to ride on a horse and lead the way.

Mr. McCabe:

I know there are not many people here. I also know we were hoping for a lot of marchers so that big business would have to take notice and finally grant us some rights. But everything has to start somewhere. Even though there are just a few of us, people will see, read, and hear our message. It may be enough to make people think. We must look toward the future and hope we make a difference today. Are you ready to march?

Group of Marchers:
Yes, let's go.

Narrator:
As the marchers lined up behind Mr. McCabe, they were excited and noisy. Their little group started down the street, proud and happy to be a part of this first Labor Day parade.

Clarice:
Father, I hear people outside. Look! There is a parade! Father, come see. What do those signs say?

Father:
Well, the first one says We Want a Labor Holiday.

Clarice:
What does that mean?

Father:
It means they want a day where people can get together and not have to work. A day where businesses and factories close. A day to spend with friends and family.

Clarice:
What does that sign say?

Father:
It says We Want Fair Pay, and the next one says We Want Shorter Work Days.

Clarice:
Why do they want shorter work days?

Father:
Some people make their employees work 15 hours a day. They want a shorter day so they can spend some time at home with their families.

Clarice:
Look at the little child carrying a sign. What does it say, Father?

Father:
It says Factories Should NOT Hire Children. I think he's right about that. Children should not have to work in factories. Looks like that's the end of the parade, Clarice.

Clarice:
That was it? Where's the music and . . . wait, Father. Listen. There is music!

Father:

I sure don't see anyone playing anything. Let's go outside and see if we can see who's playing the music.

Clarice:

Look, Father, back there. It's a big group of people. They've got a big sign, too, Father. What does it say?

Father:

It says Jewelry Workers Band.

Clarice:

Look, Father. What is that coming from the side street toward the band?

Father:

It looks like a wagon full of bricks, Clarice.

Clarice:

It is, Father. They have made something with bricks and put it in the middle of their wagon. Does their sign say Bricks?

Father:

That's close, Clarice. It says Bricklayers.

Clarice:

There are a lot of them, aren't there, Father?

Father:

There sure are, Clarice. And you know what? I think they have a good idea. I think there should be a parade. Better yet, I think we should be part of it. What do you say? Do you want to march in a parade, young lady?

Clarice:

Oh, Father. Can I? Can we?

Father:

Yes. You stay right here until I lock up the store. Then we will follow the bricklayers down the street.

Narrator:

As Clarice and Father joined the parade, others followed. It wasn't long before all of the stores were closed and people seemed to come from everywhere to march. The first Labor Day parade had started with just a few people. But by the time the parade ended at Elm Park, there were 10,000 people who had joined the parade. All around the park were people from all of the different unions and businesses, talking, laughing, and enjoying each other's company.

Clarice:

Father, look! That lady has a basket of food. Do you think if we went home and got Mother and the baby, we could bring back a basket and have a picnic, too?

Father:

I don't know why not. I'll tell you what. You stay here with your friends, and I'll go fetch Mother and the baby.

Clarice:

Father, this is going to be the best day ever. See, you and Mother were wrong! There was a parade. And better yet, we're going to have a picnic!

Father:

You know, Clarice, I think we both learned something today. You were right about the parade. Perhaps Mother and I should listen to you more often. You learned about some of the problems faced by workers, and you and I both learned what can happen when people with the same ideas get together. I'll hurry and get the family so you can tell them all about this special day.

Narrator:

From that day on, Americans have celebrated Labor Day on the first Monday in September. There are still parades and lots of picnics. Today, however, many people choose to work rather than take the day off. Although those early workers wanted people to have the day off, they were also fighting for many other rights of workers. One of those rights was choice. As a result, today some people can make a choice on Labor Day. They can work, or they can have the holiday off, just as Clarice and Father did in 1882.

Columbus, a Man Who Changed History

BACKGROUND INFORMATION

This story treats the youth of Christopher Columbus, covering the period from childhood to adulthood, and deals with his relationship with his family. Because this story covers the first 30 years of Columbus's life, it might be appropriate to assign two or three students to the part of Columbus, each portraying him at a different age. Two terms in this script may need explanation (or you may want to use them as inference questions). "The Dark Sea" was the term used by the Romans for the Atlantic Ocean. "To set and weigh anchor" means to drop and raise the anchor.

STAGING

The Narrator should stand off to one side of the performance area, while the rest of the performance should take place center stage. The actors should enter and exit the performance area as their roles indicate, using the side of the stage opposite the Narrator.

CHARACTERS

Narrator, Father, Christopher, and Bartholomew.

Columbus, a Man Who Changed History

Narrator:

Christopher Columbus was born in October of 1451. His given name was Cristóbal Colón in Spanish, and Cristoforo Colombo in Italian. Over the years, as different people wrote about him, the spelling of his name changed several times until it was spelled and pronounced as we use it today, Christopher Columbus. He was the oldest child of a large Italian family. He had one sister and two brothers who lived and one brother who died as a young child. His father was a weaver and a seller of special imported cloth. They lived in Genoa, Italy, which is a seaport. It was after working in the shop all day with his father that Christopher would spend many hours around the ships and sailors from other countries. This day was no exception as we find young Christopher leaving his father's shop.

Father:

Christopher, where are you going in such a hurry?

Christopher:

Father, a ship is coming into port today.

Father:

What is so important about this ship that you are about to leave the shop before you take off your work clothes?

Christopher:

Sorry, Father. I will change quickly. Then may I go?

Father:

Yes, Son, you may go, but you have not yet told me why this ship is so special.

Christopher:

It is coming in from the Dark Sea. No one is sure what the cargo will be. I want to see all of the cargo as it is brought off of the ship.

Father:

I am sure you will not miss a cask or trunk. Go, Christopher, but don't loose track of time. Your mother will expect you home for supper. And I will look forward to a full accounting of the cargo.

Christopher:

Yes, Father. I will see you at supper.

Narrator:

Christopher spent the rest of the daylight hours at the docks, watching with great interest as the Italian ship was being unloaded. However, as sunset came and he returned home, he was disappointed in the cargo.

Father:

Well, my son, what marvelous things did they bring back from the other side of the Dark Sea?

Christopher:

Nothing, Father. There were just the usual things from the other ports they stopped at on their way here.

Father:

Perhaps they left all of their newfound wonders at the other ports?

Christopher:

No. I talked to some of the sailors when they rested. They said they found nothing but more and more water. They think that those sailors who say they have seen land on the other side of the Dark Sea are lying for their captains. These men don't think you can get to land from the ports in France or Spain. What do you think, Father?

Father:

Perhaps they are right, Christopher, but we have seen some very unusual plants and birds when those other ships have come into port. I think hitting land must depend on which direction you sail. If the ships go another direction the next time they go into the Dark Sea, they may find these lands also. There has to be a way across the Dark Sea, Christopher.

Christopher:

Why are you so sure, Father?

Father:

When I have traveled to buy wools and yarns to make material, I have seen the water on the other side of the Orient. If you can see it is there by going one way, you should be able to get to the Orient the other way.

Christopher:

Father, you have seen the water on the other side?

Father:

Yes, I have. Would you like to go with me next time I travel and see it, too?

Christopher:
Father, may I?

Father:
I think you are old enough to travel. But you must understand, it is a very long way, and it takes a long time to get there.

Christopher:
I don't care if it takes a year. I want to go and see the Dark Sea. When do we leave?

Father:
It will be some time before we go, but I promise you when I go next, so will you.

Narrator:
Several months passed before Christopher and his father went to the Orient. Once they had gone, Christopher was sure his father was correct about being able to cross the Dark Sea from France or Spain to the Orient. He began to dream and plan for that day when he would be old enough to go to sea himself. After his return from the Orient, Christopher and his brother Bartholomew would take weekend trips with a small boat that belonged to the family. During these weekend adventures, Christopher would talk of his dreams, and Bartholomew would practice making maps of the different routes they would take around the bay to their overnight camping spots.

Christopher:
Why do you keep making these maps every time we leave port?

Bartholomew:
For practice. If I am ever going to plot your way to the Orient, I need practice. I wouldn't want to get you lost! You will need good maps to get you there. Who better to make them than I?

Christopher:
How do you plan to do that, working in a weaver's shop?

Bartholomew:
The same way you plan to sail. As soon as I am old enough, I am going to ask Father to speak to one of the mapmakers about training me. I want to tell them my ideas about maps and the stars. When they interview me, I want them to know I am prepared to study and work hard. If I take them my practice maps and can answer their questions from what I have observed, I know they will take me.

Christopher:
Have you talked to Father about this?

Bartholomew:
No. I think one dreamer is enough for him for now!

Christopher:
Ha! You may be right. I know he is not too happy with my dreams. He wants me to stay home and become a merchant like he is. I would like to be a successful merchant, but not by sitting in a shop. I can't imagine all of the treasures I could bring back and sell from the other side of the Dark Sea. Just think of the riches out there, Bartholomew.

Bartholomew:
I am sure you are right, Christopher. And just think what a team we would make! My maps, your keeping detailed diaries on where you sail. Why, together we could be the most successful team in Italy! It is an exciting thought, isn't it?

Christopher:
Bartholomew, I think it's a good idea. What kind of diaries would you need me to keep to help you make maps?

Narrator:
Bartholomew and Christopher spent many weekends talking and dreaming about their futures. Finally, the day arrived in 1469 when Christopher turned 18 and was ready to ask his father if he could leave home for his first adventure as an apprentice on an Italian ship.

Christopher:
Father, I wish to speak to you about my future.

Father:
Which future are you referring to—merchant, weaver, or sailor?

Christopher:
Father, I know you want me to stay and run this business for you when you are old. But I long to go to sea. I want to go through the Dark Sea to the Orient.

Father:
I am well aware of your dreams, Son. I do not want you to go. But then, your grandfather did not want your mother to leave Portugal to marry me, either. He was a wise man, though, and did not stop her. Therefore, I feel I must let you go and do as your heart tells you. If things do not go well, you can always come back to the shop. Yet, somehow I don't think you ever will. Is there any one ship in particular you wish to work on?

Christopher:
No, Father. Whichever one will take me is fine. Will you help me talk to a captain?

Father:
Yes, my son. Let's close the shop and go to the docks.

Christopher:
Thank you, Father.

Narrator:
For the next two years, Christopher worked hard to become the best sailor around. He was quick to learn the necessary skills. By the time he was 20, he had learned to handle, reef, and steer a ship; set and weigh an anchor; and judge distances by sight well enough that he was ready to become a seaman on a ship sailing for other parts of Europe. This would be his first trip on the Dark Sea, and it would end in tragedy.

The ship was attacked as it passed Portugal. After a valiant fight, both ships caught fire. The only chance of survival was to jump into the sea. In doing so, Columbus grabbed an oar and used it as a float, kicking his way six miles to shore. After recovering his health, Columbus went to Lisbon, Portugal, where his brother Bartholomew now lived, and assisted him in his map and chart shop.

Bartholomew:
Christopher, when are you going to tire of mapmaking and return to the sea?

Christopher:
Bartholomew, perhaps I already have. My problem is finding a sponsor so I can captain a boat rather than work for someone else. You have established yourself here. Do you know of anyone who is interested in a good captain and making a lot of money?

Bartholomew:
If you mean, do I know anyone who is willing to invest in your dream of sailing to the Orient, the answer is no. You have not made a name for yourself, yet. You need to lead a few successful trips before I can help you with your dream. But I know of a nobleman who is looking for someone to captain his fleet of ships. However, I must warn you, he will never fund your big dream.

Christopher:
Why are you so sure of that? If I can prove myself to him, perhaps I can convince him.

Bartholomew:
No, my brother. This man is out to make money on sure things. Also, he does not have the kind of money you will need for your trip to the Orient. Are you still interested?

Narrator:

With Bartholomew's help, Columbus spent several successful years sailing as far north across the Dark Sea as Iceland. During this time, Christopher married, and his first son, Diego, was born. His wife died when Diego was about five years old. Because Christopher could get no one in Portugal to fund his trip, he and Diego moved to Spain. Diego was placed in a monastery, and Columbus spent the next six years trying to convince Queen Isabella of Spain to fund his dream. He finally succeeded, and in August of 1492, Christopher Columbus finally left the Old World behind to discover a New World, reaching land in what is known to us now as the Bahamas.

Halloween

Fright Night

BACKGROUND INFORMATION

Halloween is probably one of the most unusual holidays we celebrate, as it is a mixture of Christian and pagan concepts. Because Halloween has come to be associated with black magic and elements of satanism (for example, dressing up as the Devil), many Christian groups discourage the celebration of Halloween. Therefore, it is wise to survey your class before using this material. This is a lighthearted script. It has no historical background, but it does depict a 1990s version of window painting, a Halloween custom celebrated in many small towns. This script is a little more difficult than many others, so it would be more appropriate for older students. Because the majority of the characters are male, female students should be assigned the roles of the narrator and the judges.

STAGING

The Narrator does not play a major role until the end of the reading and should therefore sit or stand to the side or the back of the room, if space is a problem. The Narrator can then move forward as the judges are evaluating the window at the end. The staging of the scenes—classroom, downtown street, window to be decorated at Sweet's store—can progress from the left of the performance area to the right. If space is limited, students can sit on stools or chairs, and stand and move forward when reading. With this second option, students would not move from the school down the street to Sweet's store. This script lends itself to a wide use of props, if the class has time to make them and you are interested in using them. Although none are essential to the script, they would add interest to the presentation.

CHARACTERS

Narrator, Mr. Manley, Evan, Kevin, Todd, Shane, Nate, Scott, Sweet, 1st Judge, and 2nd Judge.

Fright Night

Narrator:

It is the 1st of October. Mr. Manley's senior art class at East Point is coming to order. Mr. Manley has just received the guidelines for the annual Halloween competition in which students paint selected windows of downtown businesses. As in the past, there is a monetary award for the best window. Mr. Manley takes great pride in the fact that his art classes have won the top awards for the last three years, whereas Mr. Venton's classes have yet to place higher than third. The rivalry between the teachers is almost as bad as the rivalry between the students. This year, however, Mr. Manley has had a hard time keeping his class on task and is not too sure his class can win first, let alone second, place.

Mr. Manley:

All right, let's settle down. The bell has rung, so let's get it together. I have the window-painting guidelines for this year. Though they remain basically the same as every other year you have competed, this year they have cut the number of students allowed to work as a team from six to four.

Evan:

Man, you've got to be kidding! We've already worked out an idea with our group from last year. How are we gonna decide who's out of our group? This really stinks.

Kevin:

On top of that, whoever leaves our group knows our plan. Mr. M., we've got a winning window here—isn't there some way around this?

Mr. Manley:

I'm sorry, guys, but a rule's a rule. The group can be no larger than four per window.

Todd:

Well, I'm not leaving the group. This window was as much my idea as anyone else's. If I go, so does the part about the Headless Horseman.

Shane:

Shh! Can't you keep anything a secret? Mr. Manley, Kevin's right. We worked hard to put together this concept. Each of us created a piece of this window. As far as I'm concerned, either we all do it together, or none of us do it. Right, guys?

Mr. Manley:

Now come on, guys. Surely there are two of you who can work with another group. You don't even know the theme yet! How can your window be set in stone?

Nate:
Look, Mr. Manley, our window is so perfect, it'll fit any theme. You've gotta let us do this. We've spent all kinds of hours at night putting this together.

Mr. Manley:
Listen, I understand your frustration, but I can't change the rules. The committee cut the number of students per group so there would be more teams and more windows would get painted. They want to start at Neil's Best Buys and go all the way to the top of the hill. I'm sorry, guys, but I don't know what I can do to change things.

Scott:
Isn't that just like adults. If there's a way to mess things up, they sure will. Look, Mr. Manley, we know it's not your fault, but we will work as a group of six or not at all. The guys are right about that. We are a team. Last year we came in second, and we vowed we'd win first place this year if it was the last thing we did. So, somehow this has to be worked out. By the way, what is the theme this year?

Mr. Manley:
Fright Night.

Nate:
Whoa! Is that ever great, or what? I mean, our plan is perfect. Man, we've got to do our window now. There has to be a way. Hey, let's go downtown after school and scope out the place. Maybe there's an answer to our problem down there.

Shane:
Sure, why not? I can't imagine that we'll find the answer there, but it won't hurt to try. Mr. Manley, do we still get to pick our windows on a first-come basis?

Mr. Manley:
Let me see. *(Looks over the guidelines)* Hmm, well, yes, I guess you do. The committee has numbered the windows that may be painted. We have the even-numbered windows, and Mr. Vinton's class is doing the odd-numbered windows. The choices have to be in no later than the 10th, and all windows must be done by the 25th. Any other questions?

Todd:
Mr. Manley, can we stay after class and show you our sketch and why it's so important to us to do it together?

Mr. Manley:
Sure! I'd love to see it. Now do any of the rest of you have any questions? With only 20 minutes left in today's period, I want the rest of you to put your heads together and form your groups. I'd like all group lists in by tomorrow's class time. I don't want to take a lot of time putting this together. Also, don't forget, once you have your window planned, I'll need a list of the supplies you need. The sooner I get that, the better. I want to make sure I have everything long before you need it.

Narrator:
After class, the boys showed Mr. Manley their sketch. Each of them lobbied the importance of his part to the whole sketch. It wasn't long before Mr. Manley was convinced. Unfortunately, the problem remained. As the boys began their walk down Main Street, they were all a bit dejected.

Kevin:
I don't believe this has happened. I wonder who changed that stupid rule? They could just as easily have made each team do two windows rather than cutting down the size of the teams.

Todd:
What did you say?

Nate:
He said "I don't believe . . . "

Todd:
No . . . the part about two windows.

Kevin:
I don't know. I said something about us doing two windows instead of one.

Todd:
That's it! All we have to do is find a store that has two windows next to each other. We could just stretch our sketch over two windows!

Shane:
How does that help anything? We'll still have six in our group.

Todd:
Yeah, I know, but see, if we can find just the right set of windows, we could run them together. Three of us could work on one window and three on the other. Then whichever window wins, we split the prize.

Evan:

Cool! I mean, after all, it might work. Look at our sketch. It kinda breaks into two groups just by the way we brainstormed it. I think it'll work. Good thinking, Todd.

Scott:

Wrong. Our window's a total concept. You break it into two parts, and neither one of them's anything on its own. I don't see how your idea will work, Todd.

Todd:

Well, I don't know. It seems like it makes sense. Let's just see if we can find two windows that will work. Maybe Mr. Manley can solve the other part of the problem for us.

Scott:

Sure, why not? It won't hurt to consider the idea. I just wish . . .

Kevin:

There it is, Todd! Two windows right next to each other. And look, no numbers in either window. I wonder if they're going to let anyone paint their windows?

Todd:

Let's go in and check it out. It's perfect for our idea.

Nate:

Man, I don't know. Who runs this place? Any of you guys ever been in this store before? What kind of a store is named The Perplexed Cow?

Todd:

Beats me, but let's find out.

Evan:

Whoa! Check it out. Have you ever seen such . . . such stuff in your whole life? Look on that table! Those are skulls. Great junk, huh?

Kevin:

Yeah, if you're into bones and things. Guys, I really think we ought to forget this place. I mean, look over there. There are stuffed bats and owls. Oh, yuck! It's a whole case full of stuffed animals. Who'd sell real animals stuffed like that?

Sweet:

May I help you, young men?

Evan:
Hey, cool stuff! When did you open up here? I don't remember this place from before. Did you kill all of those animals and stuff them yourself? This is great! Do you really sell this stuff? How much are those . . .

Todd:
Evan, knock it off. We're here to discuss windows, not merchandise. I'm Todd, and my friends and I, we're in Mr. Manley's art class at the high school. We were looking for windows to paint for the Halloween contest. Since you have two windows right next to each other, yours would be perfect for our sketch. But we noticed you don't have any numbers on your windows. So we were wondering, did they just forget to number them, or are you not having your windows done?

Sweet:
Well, son, actually I decided to pass. The committee showed me some of the pictures they had of windows done in the past and, personally, they weren't my style. Sorry, but it would take something extra special to make me change my mind.

Shane:
Sir, I think we have just the thing for your windows, considering the interesting merchandise you sell. We happen to have a sketch of our window with us. Would you look at it and see if it might change your mind?

Narrator:
A very dubious Sweet agreed to look at the boys' sketch. Not only was he impressed with what he saw, but he had several ideas on incorporating some of his merchandise into the scene. Not sure what the limitations were, and still wondering how to pull off their scheme, the boys encouraged Sweet to see if he could get the rules for the windows changed. If three of the boys worked on each window and the two windows were judged as one, they knew they had first place made. The next afternoon, before the class bell rang, the boys were at Mr. Manley's desk finding out the limitations on materials and telling him all about their set of windows.

Evan:
This is absolutely the coolest place I've ever seen. Have you been in The Perplexed Cow, Mr. M? It has skulls, real animals that have been stuffed, this unbelievable collection of *Mad* magazines, old tin signs for Coke and Lux Soap, and an awesome body-piercing booth.

Mr. Manley:
A what?

Scott:
Evan, relax. Actually, Mr. Manley, this guy Sweet and his store are just a bit odd.

Shane:
That's putting it nicely. If it weren't for the fact that he has two windows right next to each other that are perfect for our project, I'd never set foot in that place again. It's all weird. Why would anybody collect real animals that are stuffed, or pierce people's bodies?

Todd:
Come on, guys, none of that's the point here. We have the two windows. He's agreed to let us do them, and he's trying to get the committee to agree to let the six of us do the windows if we have only three on each window. Then he's going to ask them to judge both of them together so the "total concept," as Scott calls it, is not destroyed. What we need to know is what we can and can't use along with the paints.

Mr. Manley:
What would you want to use besides paint?

Todd:
To start, we want to use one of Sweet's skulls to fix up as Ichabod Crane's head.

Mr. Manley:
Is there a hidden message behind using Ichabod Crane's head?

Shane:
What do you mean, Mr. Manley?

Mr. Manley:
Ichabod Crane was a schoolteacher before he was beheaded one fateful night. I just wondered if you had any particular teacher in mind when you thought of him . . .

Evan:
Hey, that's pretty good! But no. We just thought we'd use him because someone took his head off. Beheading's kinda cool, don't you think?

Mr. Manley:
I guess that's a matter of opinion, Evan. What else do you want to use?

Narrator:

The boys explained Sweet's other suggestions to Mr. Manley. Though he was not sure these additions were such a good idea, he had to admit it would raise the window-painting contest to a different level. After being assured Sweet's ideas would not disqualify their window, the boys spent the class time refining their sketch and putting together a list of supplies for Mr. Manley. After school they ran the distance from the high school to The Perplexed Cow to see if Sweet had gotten them permission to do the two windows and to tell Sweet he could use those certain items of his merchandise. Because the boys were doing two windows, they did get special permission to work as two groups of three. For days the boys worked on the outline of the project, painting it on the inside, rather than the outside, of Sweet's windows. On the 15th of October, Sweet covered the outside of his windows with brown paper so no one could see what the boys were doing. Each night as they worked, he was very careful to remain visible to people passing by so they would not think he was doing any of the work. Finally, on the night of October 25th, Sweet and the boys took the paper down as the judges and a crowd of curious people assembled in front of The Perplexed Cow.

1st Judge:

I thought for a moment we were here to judge the brown paper! It definitely is uniform in color.

2nd Judge:

Also unique in design! Oh, my goodness! Look at that! Why, I have never seen anything like that in my whole life.

Nate:

It's really unique, isn't it, Judge?

1st Judge:

Well, I . . . I don't know what to say. Does this meet all of the guidelines of the contest?

2nd Judge:

Yes. Granted, it's a different use of materials than we've ever seen, but it does fit the title better than any other window we've judged. As the young man said, it's unique.

1st Judge:

To say the least. I, well, this has to be the best window in our contest. Don't you agree?

2nd Judge:

No doubt about that. I just can't believe you boys did all of this work. It must have taken you every night since the 1st of October.

Kevin:

Close to it. And if Sweet had not agreed to let us do our window here, it would never have been done.

2nd Judge:

Well, congratulations, boys. You've won first prize hands down. Mr. Manley, once again your art classes have come through. I don't know how you do it, but keep it up, will you?

Narrator:

You're probably wondering what the winning window looked like. There were several things that would have made the boys' window unique even without Sweet's help. Their figures were all life-size, even the horse that Ichabod Crane rode, and the bridge seemed to span the windows as if it were real. The colors were very vibrant and unusual. The sword used to decapitate Crane glistened; the blood they painted on it seemed to be still dripping. But Sweet's additions gave the whole picture a 3-D effect that no one would ever forget. On the floor of the window display case was an array of animals from Sweet's collections—and what appeared to be a real head. The head was a modern version of Ichabod Crane and in no way resembled a typical schoolteacher of the early 1800s. When hair had been glued onto one of Sweet's skulls, it looked as though it had been cut while a bowl was held over Crane's head. The hair on top of his head stood straight up, as if he were scared. The hair was sprayed various shades of green, purple, and yellow. The facial area had been covered with some type of rubber material. Through the ears were numerous pierced earrings of all shapes and sizes. Ichabod's eye sockets had flashing red lights sunk deep into the skull cavity. But Ichabod's most unusual feature was his tongue. Twice the size of a normal tongue, it stuck out, with a barbell pierced through the center of it. There was no doubt that Sweet's body-piercing talents made this Ichabod Crane the most unforgettable ever seen in any Halloween window.

Veterans' Day

A Day of Honoring

BACKGROUND INFORMATION

Veterans' Day is celebrated on November 11th, the date the armistice was signed that ended World War I in 1918. Schools are closed, and many children view the holiday merely as a day away from the classroom. This script will help them understand that there is more to Veterans' Day than simply being out of school. Veterans' Day was originally celebrated only at Arlington National Cemetery in Virginia, where the president of the United States and other officials would place a wreath on the Tomb of the Unknown Soldier to honor World War I veterans. The holiday was known as Armistice Day until February 1954, when its name was changed to Veterans' Day. It was not until June 1, 1954, that President Dwight D. Eisenhower signed the Veterans' Day holiday into law. Previously, different states had celebrated it as a state legal holiday.

STAGING

The Narrator should stand to the left of the staging area, and the other readers should sit center stage. Because this script has only male readers, the Narrator should be a girl.

CHARACTERS

Narrator, Andrew, Jack, Eddie, and Hank.

A Day of Honoring

Narrator:
In January of 1954 in Emporia, Kansas, Edward Rees and a group of friends are discussing the way that people in the United States remember those soldiers who have served their country in time of war. They feel that not everyone takes time to think back on the wars that have occurred, the lives lost, and the injuries of those who gave of themselves to assure freedom for the world.

Andrew:
I was really disappointed in last year's Armistice Day events. Seems like no one really comes out or cares about those of us who fought in the wars overseas.

Jack:
Yeah, I know what you mean. We're really behind the times here in Emporia. Look at the District of Columbia. For years they've given people the day off from work, and they put on a big parade and celebration at Arlington National Cemetery, where so many soldiers are buried.

Eddie:
Sure, but Arlington National Cemetery and the Tomb of the Unknown Soldier are right there. It's easy for them to have a big event.

Hank:
But we've got soldiers buried in our cemetery. And we've got plenty of men here who fought in the last two wars. I don't see why we can't have a big parade and a celebration at the cemetery here, too.

Jack:
How do you think you're going to make that happen? Everyone views this as a holiday only for the veterans of World War I. We've got to change the way people view the holiday. Eddie's the only one I know who can help.

Eddie:
What do you mean? I don't have anything to do with what goes on here in Emporia. I'm a U.S. representative in Washington, not a state representative in Kansas.

Andrew:
Who says things need to change only in Kansas?

Eddie:
What do you mean?

Andrew:
Why shouldn't the change be a national change and recognize all of the veterans from all of the wars? The way the holiday is viewed now, nothing special really happens in lots of towns.

Eddie:
The president has always told people to celebrate the holiday as they see fit. Any city or state can make it a legal holiday and honor whomever they want.

Jack:
Sure, but how many do? Let's face it, if Washington doesn't pass a bill to make some change in the way we view Armistice Day all across America, it'll never happen. No one's gonna take the bull by the horns in every city and make the holiday the kind of tribute it should be.

Hank:
Jack's right about that. If we were disappointed, imagine how many other veterans feel the same? I think you're right, Andrew. I think the day needs to be a tribute to all veterans. People ought to remember all of the men and women who have served their country.

Jack:
And just think of all the people who didn't come back as healthy as we did. We were lucky. We've still got all of our limbs, and we have our families to support us. Just think how many came back crippled. And for some of them, their families didn't stick by them. They need the support of other Americans to know that what they gave up was worth it.

Eddie:
You're right. Some of them did pay an awful price for fighting over there. Remember Bert? He lost both legs and then spent three years in the hospital.

Andrew:
Yeah, but the worst part was losing his wife and three kids. I guess I can't blame her, in a way. He really was not himself once he got hurt. But still, to just leave him like that to take care of himself. That's tough on everyone.

Jack:
Well, maybe she'd have stuck by him if she'd known he wouldn't live very long.

Hank:

Oh, that's no excuse. Anyway, who did stick by him and others like him? Sometimes even we didn't do what we could for him. It's people like that—and families who lost loved ones—who need to be remembered and honored. Sure, we fought and it was rough. But now we need to make people remember the others.

Andrew:

You've got to help us, Eddie. You represent us in Washington. We want you to do just that and present a bill to make Armistice Day a holiday for all veterans from all wars that have been fought.

Hank:

I'm with you, Andrew. What do you say, Eddie? Will you write a bill and present it to Congress?

Eddie:

I don't know how much support I'll get, but you've convinced me to do it. I may have to bring you guys to Washington to convince everyone else, though.

Andrew:

I don't think it'll be that hard. I bet there isn't anyone in Congress who doesn't know someone who died or was maimed in the wars in Europe. I bet you can get that bill passed the first time you propose it.

Jack:

And if you have any resistance, just remind them they wouldn't be in Congress today if it weren't for the soldiers who fought for their freedom to be elected and represent the people. I just know it'll pass. Then this year on November 11, instead of just a few people remembering the soldiers, maybe everyone will. While you're at it, the day probably needs a new name. People associate Armistice Day only with World War I. A new name might make it more important to everyone.

Eddie:

That could be tricky. I think we'd better come up with one before I present the bill. Anyone have any suggestions?

Jack:

Make it simple. Why not just call it Veterans' Day? It's supposed to be a day to remember the dead, but by calling it Veterans' Day, it can also be a day to remember the living veterans.

Hank:

Especially the soldiers in the hospitals. All of us, alive, handicapped, and dead, should be remembered and honored.

Eddie:

As soon as I go back to Washington next month, I'll present the bill to Congress. It'll be a great victory for the veteran if Congress agrees.

Narrator:

In February of 1954, Edward H. Rees presented his bill to Congress. From that day on, Armistice Day was officially known as Veterans' Day to honor all who had fought and would fight in any war in Europe or elsewhere in the world.

Thanksgiving Blues*

BACKGROUND INFORMATION

Arney is the only fifth-grader in a one-room schoolhouse. It is the day before Thanksgiving, and the class is singing as a group. There are 13 students in the school, and they are all excited about Thanksgiving break, except for Arney. Because many children will be unfamiliar with the concept of a one-room schoolhouse, it would be a good idea to discuss the idea with students beforehand.

STAGING

This script is somewhat difficult to stage because there are so many different scenes. The Narrator will need to stand off to the side of the performance area. The school scene should take place to one side, the farmyard scene in the center, and the river scene on the other side. Simple props would be helpful, such as desks for the school, a tree for the yard, and some blue paper to indicate water. A stuffed toy dog would make a good prop for the final scene.

CHARACTERS

Narrator, Mrs. Cornwell, Christine, Ruth, Greta, Arney, Dad, and Mom. Option: If you have a large class, you could assemble a total of 13 students to represent the class and have them actually sing the various songs as they are suggested or incorporate your own choice of music.

*Adapted from Aileen Fisher, "Thanksgiving Blues," in *It's Time for Thanksgiving*, edited by Elizabeth Hough Sechrist and Janette Woolsey (Philadelphia, Pa.: MacRae Smith, 1957). Adapted with permission from Aileen Fisher.

Thanksgiving Blues

Narrator:

The school day was almost over. Because the next day was Thanksgiving, Mrs. Cornwell decided everyone would join in singing rather than working on various subjects. She knew one of her students, Arney, really wasn't interested in working because he was upset about the death of his dog, Skip. Skip had been Arney's dog for ages, but he had gotten old and died, and Arney really missed him a lot. Mrs. Cornwell thought the singing might help cheer Arney up. The class started out with "Over the River and Through the Woods." Because it was the only Thanksgiving song they knew, the first-graders wanted to sing it over and over again. Arney tried to sing along, but he could not keep his mind off of Skip.

Mrs. Cornwell:

Now that we have sung "Over the River" twice, who can suggest another song we can all sing?

Christine:

Let's sing "Oh, Suzanna." *(All join in the singing)*

Mrs. Cornwell:

My, you certainly sang a rousing version of that. Is there another song someone else would like to sing? Ruth?

Ruth:

I'd like to sing "My Old Kentucky Home." *(Again, the whole class sings)*

Mrs. Cornwell:

I must say, you are all in fine voice today. I don't know when I've heard you sing so well. Is there one last song anyone would like to sing? Greta?

Greta:

Mrs. Cornwell, is there another Stephen Foster song you could teach us? I really like his music.

Mrs. Cornwell:

Why, yes. We could learn "Jeanie with the Light Brown Hair." I'll hum the tune for you and then sing it for you.

Narrator:

Arney had long ago quit singing. The music made him sadder instead of happy. And when Mrs. Cornwell began singing about dreaming of Jeanie, all he could think about were his dreams of Skip. When school was over. Arney stayed after to help Mrs. Cornwell clean the room. He didn't feel like going home just yet, and he definitely wasn't up to walking with everybody else.

Mrs. Cornwell:

I hope you're going to have a nice Thanksgiving, Arney.

Arney:

I don't think so.

Mrs. Cornwell:

Greta told me about Skip. I'm so sorry you lost your friend.

Arney:

I think I'll empty out the water bucket so it won't freeze over vacation.

Mrs. Cornwell:

Thank you for helping me, Arney. Work always goes faster when you have someone to share it with.

Arney:

That's how it always was when Skip was around. Now nothing's any fun anymore. Bye, Mrs. Cornwell.

Narrator:

By the time Arney caught up with his sisters Greta and Christine, they were almost home. From the end of the lane, they could see their father's truck in the yard. Excited to find out where their folks had been, the girls ran ahead of Arney. By the time Arney finally got to the truck, he could see Greta jumping up and down excitedly.

Greta:

Arney, hurry! Come see what is in this box. Hurry! Hurry!

Dad:

I brought you something from Caxton's, Son. She's a little timid because she's not had much attention. Never had a ride in a truck before, either.

Greta:

Hurry up, Arney! Dad, can I get her out of the box?

Dad:

No, you'd better let me get her. She's pretty scared. Son, it was tough luck losing Skipper right before vacation. I thought you might be glad to have another dog. She's a good one, and you can train her all by yourself.

Mom:

Isn't she cute? She's so young. What do you think of her?

Arney:

She's all right, I guess. But she's not Skipper.

Dad:

No, she's not, Son. She's just a little puppy. In time she'll grow up, though. But if you don't want her, I can take her back to Caxton's. It's up to you, Son.

Arney:

I don't know, Dad. Skip was so special. Remember the time he saved me when I fell into the stream? He was big and strong. She's just a little thing. What good will she ever be?

Mom:

Well, that's hard to tell, Arney. Right now she's scared to death and so little. Maybe if you give her a chance, you'll learn to love her, too.

Arney:

I don't know how. Well, let's see if there's anything you can do. Come on girl! Let's go walk down to the stream.

Narrator:

As hard as the puppy tried, she was either underneath Arney's feet or lagging so far behind that Arney would have to stop and wait for her. He thought she was a real pain. As they got closer to the stream, Arney's memories of Skipper grew stronger and stronger. Arney started to walk on the top of the rocks in the stream. He had forgotten all about the puppy. When he finally remembered her, he tried to get her to come out onto the rocks with him, as Skipper had done. He didn't think about how small the puppy was. After Arney urged the puppy to jump on the rocks several times, the puppy tried, but she slipped on some ice. Before Arney knew what had happened, the puppy had fallen into the cold water. Arney rushed back to pull her out of the icy water. He ran home with the puppy zipped inside of his jacket.

Dad:

Arney, where's your puppy?

Arney:

Oh, the poor little tyke. She fell into the stream. I put her inside my coat so she could warm up. I guess I'll keep her. I think she needs me to make sure she grows up safely. And Mom's right, she is sorta cute.

Dad:

What are you going to name her?

Arney:

Jeanie.

Dad:

Jeanie? Why Jeanie?

Arney:

Because she's got light brown hair just like the Jeanie Mrs. Cornwell sang about today.

Native American Heritage Day

The Legend of Yellow Hair*

BACKGROUND INFORMATION

Native Americans have played a major role in the history of the United States. In many schools, Native American Heritage Day is celebrated the week after Thanksgiving. There is no set date for this observance. This historical script is included for teachers who wish to recognize the Native American. It is based on the Battle of the Little Big Horn, the greatest—and nearly the only—battle fought by the Confederation of Plains Indian tribes. The confederation included the Sioux, Cheyenne, and Arapaho Indians, who had joined together in an attempt to run the whites off of the plains and sacred areas of the Black Hills of the Dakotas and Devil's Tower in Wyoming. General George Armstrong Custer, whom the Indians called Yellow Hair, led the Seventh Calvary in battle against the Indians at Little Big Horn. What really happened at that battle remains unclear, but in the end, Yellow Hair died, leaving behind a white wife, as well as a son from a bigamous marriage with a Cheyenne woman.

This script represents the Native American version of the events surrounding the Battle of the Little Big Horn. The retelling is based on the events as told to Alice Marriott and Carol K. Rachlen by Mary Little Bear Inkanish and John Stands-in-the-Timber, and by John Fletcher, all from the Cheyenne tribe, and as told to them by Richard Pratt, from the Arapaho Indian tribe. This script recounts one of the sadder moments in American history, during a period in which many Indians were sacrificed in the many wars between the Indians and white men. This story describes not only the devastation, but also the clever minds of the Indians as they planned the downfall of their worst enemy, General Custer.

For some classrooms this story may not be suitable. The teacher will have to consider the ethnic makeup of the class, as well as the ability of the students to understand this tragic event. It is advised that the teacher spend time reading about and discussing this event before students prepare the script. This will help resolve any difficulties with the content. This story, told from the Native-American viewpoint, is included to show that General Custer, whom history books often portray as a victim, may have actually received just punishment for his betrayal of the Indians at the Washita River, an attack not sanctioned by the army.

The dialogue between Custer and his men before the Washita River attack and at Fort Abraham Lincoln before the last battle is my creation; all other dialogue and details are from the story as it was retold.

---

*Adapted from Alice Marriott and Carol K. Rachlen, "Yellow Hair: George Armstrong Custer," in *American Indian Mythology* (New York: Thomas Y. Crowell, 1968).

Because the first narration is very long, the teacher may want to present the first two paragraphs as an introduction before the reading; in this case, the Narrator's opening speech would begin with the third paragraph, "In 1871 . . . ." If the first narration is left intact, it should be divided among two or three Narrators so the listeners do not become bored. This script can involve a large number of students and is therefore a good candidate to prepare and present to another class or to parents. It can easily accommodate the whole class. Because all but one of the speaking roles are male, a female Narrator is recommended (in fact, the narration can be divided among a series of female Narrators). Girls can also be assigned to perform as soldiers and Indians during the battle.

STAGING

The Narrator is significant in this script and therefore should stand front left. Center stage should be reserved for the battles; all other scenes should take place on the right side of the staging area. Stools or chairs should be assembled stage right for the peace treaty meeting between Custer and the Indian chiefs. Those readers involved in the first scene should already be assembled during the opening narration. Action during the narration of the presentation of the peace pipe would enhance the production, as the Narrator's speech is quite long. The same is true during the battle scenes. Students should always enter and exit the staging area during the narration.

EXTENSION ACTIVITIES

This script presents a fantastic opportunity for the class to research and speculate on a number of unanswered questions. Two obvious questions are, What happened to Custer's son? and Why was Keogh's horse, Comanche, left alive? The first question makes a wonderful open-ended writing assignment in which students project their ideas about Custer's son's life after his mother's death. The reasons for Comanche's survival would make an excellent study into the beliefs of the Indians and how they honor not only humans and animals, but all parts of our environment.

CHARACTERS

Narrator, Black Kettle, 1st Chief, 2nd Chief, General Custer (Yellow Hair), Major Eliot, Sergeant Adams, General Terry, Elizabeth Custer, Tom Custer, Captain Keogh, and soldiers and Indians as determined to enhance the performance. A messenger will be necessary if the option of acting out the first scene during the narration is used.

The Legend of Yellow Hair

Narrator:

In the 1870s, the United States Army ran Fort Abraham Lincoln in South Dakota as an outpost dealing with Indian affairs. One of the army's generals at this fort was George Custer. He was very involved with the peace treaties and relationships between the Indians and the United States government, as well as Indian relations with the army. Many of us have heard the white man's side of the story of General Custer and the Battle of the Little Big Horn. In most of these stories, General Custer is viewed as a hero and victim. He is often seen as a hero because he was able to make peace treaties between the Indians and whites when no one else could. Because he lost his life fighting the Indians at Little Big Horn, many have felt he was the victim of this cruel war. However, there are two sides to the story.

This presentation is based on retellings describing the relationship between General Custer, whom the Indians called Yellow Hair, and the Indians, from the Indians' point of view. You will meet a General Custer who is very different from what you might expect. In this story, you will find out that General Custer was not a real friend of the Indians. He often killed them for no reason. When he himself was killed, it was at the hands of angry Indians who were getting even for the cruel things he had done. The Indians do not see General Custer as a hero. Rather, he is someone they could not trust.

In 1871, General Custer had been at peace treaty talks at Medicine Lodge Creek, South Dakota. However, the Indians did not trust Yellow Hair. He had taken both an Indian wife and a white wife, which the Indians did not think was right. They knew he would disobey the army's orders when he was told to stay at the fort with his wife. Instead, he would go to his Indian wife's teepee and stay with her people. He was known to lie to the Indians, and he would not take care of his own half-Indian son. The Indians, knowing all of this, decided to ask General Custer to a special peace talk at Black Kettle's teepee in 1872. Black Kettle, the chief of the Cheyenne, and two chiefs from the Arapaho tribe had a feast with Yellow Hair. After the feast, a young messenger brought in a special bag that contained a T-shaped pipe of red pipestone with a dogwood stem. After Chief Black Kettle assembled the pipe, he filled it with native tobacco mixed with sumac bark. Using a coal from the fire, he lit the pipe. As was the Indian tradition, he blew smoke to Maheo above, to Mother Earth, and to the four corners of the world before addressing Yellow Hair and the other Indian chiefs.

Black Kettle:

Yellow Hair, we have called you to our council because we want to make peace and keep the peace. We have set our marks on paper, but that is the white man's way. Now we ask you to swear the peace the Indian way, too. Smoke with us, Yellow Hair.

Narrator:

The Indians knew Yellow Hair never smoked. Even smelling tobacco smoke made him ill. However, Yellow Hair knew his success and advancement depended on his control of the Indians. Yellow Hair took the pipe, and following Black Kettle's lead, six times he puffed smoke in the six different directions. With this action, he agreed to the terms of the peace.

Black Kettle:

Yellow Hair, you have smoked with us. You have promised us peace in our tradition. Now you may go.

Narrator:

After Custer had left the teepee, Black Kettle shook the dottle out of the pipe and into the palm of his hand. He then sprinkled a pinch of dottle into each heel print.

Black Kettle:

Yellow Hair has gone. Hear me, my chiefs. If he breaks the promise he has made with us today, he will die. His death will be a coward's death. No Indian is to soil his hands with Yellow Hair's scalp.

1st Chief:

So be it!

2nd Chief:

Hah-ho! If Yellow Hair breaks the promise he has sworn in the peace treaty, then let him die a coward's death.

Narrator:

Two years later, the Cheyenne and Arapaho had camped on the banks of the Washita River for the winter. Until this time, peace had been kept between the Indians and the white men. General Custer and his men were at Fort Abraham Lincoln. Upon learning of the movement of the Indian camps to the river, Custer saw his opportunity to attack the Indians and weaken them. To put his plan into action, he called Major Eliot into his office.

General Custer:

Major Eliot, the Indian camps are split: the Cheyenne are camped upriver from the Arapaho. We will split into two groups to match them. Major, you will lead a detachment to attack the Arapaho, and I'll lead a detachment against the Cheyenne.

Major Eliot:

Why do you want to attack now? It is bitter cold out there.

General Custer:
That is exactly why I want to attack now. The Indians will stay inside the teepees to stay out of the cold. There will be little resistance to our efforts. We should be able to wipe them out with no trouble, and with few losses on our side.

Major Eliot:
When do you want to attack?

General Custer:
We will assemble and ride out at first light. We should be in position to attack at midnight two days from now. We will want to hit both camps at once; if we do not, our gunshots at the first camp may alert the second, and we'll lose our advantage. Do you have any other questions, Major?

Major Eliot:
No, Sir. I'll prepare the troops.

Narrator:
Both the Cheyenne and Arapaho camps were attacked as planned. Custer's men destroyed the Cheyenne camp. Black Kettle died holding the United States flag he had been given at the Medicine Lodge peace treaty signing. No one was left alive. Everything was burned, except for the items the Seventh Calvary troops took for themselves. As daylight approached, the troops went into the Indian pasture and shot the great herds of horses. Meanwhile, it was strangely quiet at the Arapaho camp.

General Custer:
Sergeant Adams, I want you to take a small group of men down to the Arapaho camp and help Major Eliot finish up there. As soon as possible, have Major Eliot bring his detachment back here so we can form up and return to Fort Abraham Lincoln.

Sergeant Adams:
Yes, Sir. Should we take anything extra with us, Sir?

General Custer:
No, just your rifles and ammunition. You won't be there long.

Narrator:
Upon arriving at the Arapaho camp, Sergeant Adams and his detachment were shocked to find all of the soldiers in Major Eliot's detachment dead. Before the Arapaho left, they had scalped all of the men, including Major Eliot. When Custer returned to the fort, burdened with this news, his action and the resulting loss of men was met with a stern reprisal: He was sent back East for one year. While Custer was in the East, his Cheyenne wife died of grief caused by Custer's attack on her people. His Indian son was hidden from Custer by her sisters to be raised as a Cheyenne. Meanwhile, the

Cheyenne planned their revenge for Yellow Hair's attack on Black Kettle and his camp. Crow and Pawnee Indians reported to General Terry at Fort Abraham Lincoln that Cheyenne, Arapaho, and Sioux tribes were gathering in camps along the Little Big Horn and Tongue rivers. They were preparing to attack the fort and white settlers. Custer, who had returned to the fort, was summoned by General Terry to discuss the situation.

General Terry:
Custer, there is a great deal of movement of a number of Indian tribes. They seem to be settling in along the Little Big Horn and Tongue rivers. We have been advised they are preparing to attack. We must attack them first. We will split our regiment into three detachments. You will lead one, and Major Reno and I will each lead one of the other two. We will surround the camps on the Little Big Horn and attack.

General Custer:
Who will ride with me?

General Terry:
You may make that decision. Do you have a preference?

General Custer:
Sir, if I may, I would like my brother Tom and his troops, along with Captain Myles Keogh and his men, to accompany me. I have a great deal of confidence in these two officers, Sir. I know they will do as I command.

General Terry:
Fine. Just remember, Custer, I am in charge, and you are to act according to my orders.

General Custer:
Yes, Sir. When do we leave, Sir?

General Terry:
In two days. It will take that long to assemble the provisions.

General Custer:
We will be ready to leave when you wish, Sir. If you will excuse me now, I will begin my arrangements.

Narrator:
The night before they were to leave, Custer, Tom, and Myles Keogh dined together at Custer's quarters with Custer's wife, Elizabeth. After dinner and much discussion about the upcoming attack, the men made a rash move to clip off all of their hair.

Elizabeth:

I can't believe you are doing this! Why do you insist upon going into battle bald?

Tom:

Elizabeth, the Indians know George by his yellow hair. If the three of us clip off our hair, it may not be as easy to tell which one of us is George.

Captain Keogh:

Plus, this way the Indians will take less joy in saying they scalped the great General Custer.

Elizabeth:

You say that as if you think you are going to die!

Captain Keogh:

Isn't that the feeling of most people at the fort? Be honest Elizabeth, there are few here who expect us to win this battle.

Elizabeth:

If that is true, then why are you putting yourselves in such danger?

Tom:

If the Crow and Pawnee are right, the Indian confederation will attack us. I'd much rather die attacking than be the victim of an Indian attack.

Elizabeth:

I don't know how you can be sure these Crow and Pawnee are telling you the truth. What if it is all lies just to get you into a losing battle?

General Custer:

Elizabeth, these men are our scouts. They are well taken care of to provide us with useful information about the other tribes. They have never lied to us in the past, so there is no reason to suspect they would do so now.

Elizabeth:

I still don't understand why you trust them, regardless of what you say. I don't like the idea of your walking into a trap and never returning.

General Custer:

Elizabeth, have no fear. I have always returned from my dealings with the Indians. This time will be no different.

Narrator:

While the Crow and Pawnee knew of the plans of the other Indians, the Cheyenne, Sioux, and Arapaho knew of General Terry's plans. On a sunny morning in July, General Terry led the men from the fort to sure death. General Custer and his men were driven back onto a steep hill while trying to attack the Cheyenne. Slowly and methodically, the Indians killed Custer and all of his detachment. Major Reno's men, who were further downstream, were pinned down by the Arapaho. While the battle raged, the Indian women broke camp and moved back into the Black Hills to await their victorious warriors.

Once General Terry rescued Major Reno and his detachment, he found Custer and his men slaughtered. The only living being on the hill was Captain Keogh's horse, Comanche. To this day no one knows for sure whether Yellow Hair was recognized by the Cheyenne warriors, but it is clear he died a coward. His body remained intact, while all other bodies had been scalped. He lay on his back with a woman's knife thrust through his heart.

Hanukkah

The Magic Mirror of Rabbi Adam*

BACKGROUND INFORMATION

This folktale tells of a meeting between good and evil. Evil, in this case, is a sorcerer out to take another man's wife, and good is a rabbi who has a mirror with magical powers. The rabbi and the sorcerer are pitted against each other in a contest that will determine the fate of a man, the husband of the woman the sorcerer wishes to marry.

STAGING

Because this is an all-male cast, a female Narrator is suggested; as her part is quite prominent, she needs to be positioned at the front, to one side. The meeting of the Merchant and Rabbi Adam in the first scene should take place to the other side of the performance area, and center stage should be used for the contest between Rabbi Adam and the Sorcerer. In staging the contest, the Noblemen and Merchant should arrange their stools or chairs in a semicircle behind a table or desks facing the audience, and Rabbi Adam and the Sorcerer should work in the center of the semicircle, playing alternately toward the Noblemen and the audience for effect. Because the contest scene calls for action, the Sorcerer and Rabbi Adam should stand and act out the various movements as the Narrator speaks. This is an excellent script for mime. During the mime sequence, if you choose to include one, the Sorcerer and Rabbi Adam can place their scripts on the table in front of the Noblemen.

CHARACTERS

Narrator, Rabbi Adam, Man, Merchant, Merchant's Friend, Innkeeper, Sorcerer, 1st Nobleman, 2nd Nobleman, 3rd Nobleman, Friends or Noblemen added to the script at the teacher's discretion.

---

*Adapted from a Jewish folktale found in Jane Yolen, "The Magic Mirror of Rabbi Adam," in *Favorite Folktales from Around the World* (New York: Random House, 1986).

The Magic Mirror of Rabbi Adam

Narrator:

Rabbi Adam possessed a magic mirror that had once belonged to King David. With this mirror, he could see things that took place all over the world. One day, he looked into this mirror and saw that a Jew in a certain city was in mortal danger, although he had done nothing to deserve this fate. Quickly, Rabbi Adam went to the city to find the Jew and assist him. Upon arriving in the marketplace, the rabbi found a large crowd of people.

Rabbi Adam:

My good man, why are so many people crowded together here?

Man:

Throughout most of the year, the city is quiet and subdued. But for two weeks each year, it seethes like a boiling pot, and merchants come from all corners of the land to sell their wares.

Narrator:

The rabbi continued through the city until he came to a tavern. There he found the Jewish merchant he had seen in his mirror. He approached the man and spoke to him.

Rabbi Adam:

Pay heed, for when four hours have passed, you will be killed.

Narrator:

Now, the merchant thought the rabbi was mad, so he did not even speak. He continued to eat his lunch. When he was finished, he crossed the room to tell some fellow merchants what the rabbi had said. They agreed the rabbi must be mad, and they made light of the whole situation. An hour passed, and the rabbi returned to speak to the merchant.

Rabbi Adam:

Know that the hours of your life are short. You have only three hours left to live.

Narrator:

Again, the merchant and his friends laughed at the rabbi's warning. The merchant returned to the market to sell his wares. When the next hour was up, again the rabbi came to warn the merchant of his impending death.

Rabbi Adam:

One hour ago, I spoke to you, and your mouth was filled with laughter. Now there are only two hours left in your life.

Narrator:
This time the rabbi frightened the merchant, who sought the counsel of his friends.

Merchant:
He came again, this rabbi. He told me I have but two hours left to live.

Merchant's Friend:
Why didn't you stop him before he left? Perhaps he is plotting to kill you!

Merchant:
If he returns, I will not let him go until he tells me everything. But I am convinced he intends me no harm.

Narrator:
One more hour passed, and again Rabbi Adam came to the merchant with his warning.

Rabbi Adam:
Know that in one hour you will leave this world.

Merchant:
Wait! You must not leave until you tell me everything you know about me. Who are you, and who is plotting to kill me?

Rabbi Adam:
You have spoken truly. There are those who are plotting to kill you. I have discovered this plot and come to warn you. My only wish is to save you from descending into the grave.

Merchant:
If this is the case, tell me what I should do.

Rabbi Adam:
Come with me and do everything I command.

Merchant:
I am ready to follow you.

Rabbi Adam:
Let us go and speak to the innkeeper.

Merchant:
Let's go quickly, if my time is so short.

Rabbi Adam:
Innkeeper, how much money do you earn each day at the inn?

Innkeeper:
Twenty silver shekels a day.

Rabbi Adam:
If that is so, behold! I am giving you 20 shekels on the condition that you do not allow anyone else to enter your inn for the rest of the day, neither to eat nor to drink. Nor must you allow any wagon drivers to rest in your courtyard.

Innkeeper:
As you wish, Rabbi.

Narrator:
The innkeeper heeded his words and closed the inn. After this, Rabbi Adam turned to the innkeeper's servant and requested a bathtub be brought to the merchant's room and filled with water. When the tub was ready, the rabbi instructed the merchant to undress and get into the tub. Upon doing so, the rabbi gave the merchant the magic mirror.

Rabbi Adam:
Tell me what you see in the mirror.

Merchant:
I see my wife in the company of a townsman who is known to be a sorcerer. They are sitting together, eating and drinking and hugging and kissing. On the table is a bow and arrow.

Rabbi Adam:
Know that your wife has betrayed you with the evil sorcerer. Even now, they are plotting your death. The danger is very great, for the sorcerer has the powers of evil at his command. These powers will guide the arrow he shoots so that it pierces your heart. Once you are dead, they intend to marry. With the help of God, this evil plan will not succeed. Now look again and tell me what you see in the mirror.

Merchant:
Your words are true. The sorcerer is making ready to shoot the arrow.

Rabbi Adam:
Do not be afraid or let your heart be faint, for there is no turning back. When you see him shoot the arrow, put your head underwater at once. You must hold your breath and remain submerged until the arrow has passed you by and gone astray. I will signal you to lift your head.

Narrator:

And the merchant did just as he was told. A few seconds after he had submerged his head in the water, a sound like the hissing of an arrow was heard in the room. When it was gone, Rabbi Adam shouted to the merchant to lift his head out of the water. The rabbi then made the merchant look into the mirror once more and tell him what he saw.

Merchant:

My wife is in a black mood, and the sorcerer's spirit is raging within him.

Rabbi Adam:

Good. Now watch closely and see if he sends forth another arrow. If he does, do as you did before.

Narrator:

Again the merchant submerged himself in the water as an arrow hissed passed his tub. The rabbi told the merchant to watch for the arrow a third time. If the sorcerer shot a third arrow, the rabbi instructed him to leave the little finger of his right hand out of the water as he submerged the rest of his body. It was not long before the third arrow was released and the merchant submerged himself again, exposing just a fingertip. The merchant felt a sharp pain sting his finger, and his hand fell back into the tub. When the merchant emerged from the water, Rabbi Adam handed him the mirror and asked what he saw.

Merchant:

The sorcerer and my wife are rejoicing, but why? I am still alive.

Rabbi Adam:

It is because they have been deceived into thinking the arrow has killed you. Your finger stopped the arrow and did not permit it to pass through the inn as the first two had done. Now you may dress. So far you have been saved, but danger still lingers around you. Do not be afraid. I will tell you what to do to save your life.

Narrator:

The next day the merchant returned to his own city. But following the rabbi's instructions, he went to the home of a relative. He remained there for three weeks, hiding from all he knew. At the end of three weeks, he went to the marketplace. When the sorcerer saw him, the sorcerer became very pale, then approached the merchant.

Sorcerer:

It has been said in town that you were in your grave.

Merchant:

I was saved from an early grave.

Sorcerer:
Who saved you?

Merchant:
A holy man. Rabbi Adam is his name.

Sorcerer:
If you do not bring this man to me, you will surely die.

Merchant:
He said he would gladly meet you. Fix a time and place, and I will send for him.

Narrator:
The meeting between the rabbi and the sorcerer was set for the sorcerer's home. The sorcerer was so sure he could beat the rabbi that he invited all of the nobles of the province to witness the contest. When the merchant and rabbi arrived, they found the men quite drunk.

1st Nobleman:
Perform wonders for us, Rabbi. Show us your powers!

Rabbi Adam:
I do not perform wonders, but I put my faith and trust in the Lord. His power has never failed me.

Narrator:
The noblemen were not fond of the rabbi, and this response only made them angrier. They demanded the sorcerer begin the contest. Taking a bowl filled with water, the sorcerer passed his staff over the bowl, and the water disappeared. He passed his staff over the bowl a second time, and the water reappeared. He handed the bowl to the rabbi who easily accomplished the same feat. The rabbi then passed his hand back over the bowl a third time. When the noblemen looked into the bowl, they found the rabbi had turned the water to wine. The sorcerer was furious. He took down a cage in which he kept a dove and placed the dove on the table. Passing his staff over the dove, the dove dropped to the table, dead. Passing his staff over the dove again, the dove stood and began flapping its wings. The rabbi accepted the challenge. After rendering the dove dead, he waved his hand over the dove and it arose and flew around the room. It then landed on the table, laying an egg that cracked open as a small fledgling appeared.

Sorcerer:
Rabbi, you have matched or outdone me on both tries. But I have one more feat to perform that I am sure you cannot duplicate. You must leave the room while I do the trick, however, for I do not want you to overhear the spell.

Rabbi Adam:
As you wish, Sorcerer.

Narrator:
After the rabbi had gone, the sorcerer held his staff in the center of the room and pronounced a spell over it. The staff began to produce blossoms and branches, followed by leaves and apples. The noblemen were astonished at the sorcerer's feat. They called the rabbi back into the room.

Sorcerer:
Before you is my staff, blossoming as a tree. Now let us see how great your power is. Can you change this tree back into my staff?

Rabbi Adam:
Since the master of the house commanded me to leave the room while he performed his magic spell, I make the same request.

Narrator:
The noblemen agreed that this was a fair request, and the sorcerer left the room. The rabbi walked around the tree seven times saying:

Rabbi Adam:
How good are these apples and how pleasant this tree. Honored sir *(turning toward the 2nd Nobleman)*, would you be so kind as to cut off this very red apple at the top of the tree?

2nd Nobleman:
With pleasure.

Narrator:
As soon as the nobleman had cut off the apple, the tree began to wither. The blossoms, leaves, branches, and all of the apples fell off. All that remained was the staff and the one apple that the nobleman had cut off. The rabbi sent one of the noblemen to bring in the sorcerer. But the nobleman returned alone.

Rabbi Adam:
Where is the sorcerer?

3rd Nobleman:
Rabbi, his body is crumbled in one corner of the room and his head is in another. What has happened?

Rabbi Adam:

Whoever undertakes to perform magic puts his life at risk. Every wonder created contains one weakness that can undo the magician.

Narrator:

The noblemen thought hard on the rabbi's words and agreed the sorcerer had put himself at risk by asking the rabbi to undo his magic. The rabbi left the noblemen with great honor. The merchant rejoiced over the rabbi's miracles.

Merchant:

Again, thank you for saving my life, Rabbi.

Rabbi Adam:

Give thanks to God, not me. All great miracles come from Him. It is the Lord's desire that only good be used in the lives of man, not evil. Evil deeds ruin man's life, while good deeds are the way of the righteous.

The Christmas Tree*

BACKGROUND INFORMATION

This script, a story about the meaning of gift-giving, features animal characters and is geared for younger students to perform. However, it provides an excellent example of anthropomorphism, and if you are explaining this concept to junior-high-level students, they might enjoy presenting this reading to a lower grade, if there is one in the building.

STAGING

The Narrator should stand to the back of the performance area. As the scene opens, the characters stand at the front of the stage in their various groupings, with Mr. and Mrs. Rabbit far to one side. As they leave their home, Mr. and Mrs. Rabbit will walk across the stage and pick up the other characters in the following order: first Cat, then Black Hen, Goose, Pig, and Cow, and, finally, Mr. Giraffe and Mr. Lion, who are at the Christmas tree. Each character except Mr. Giraffe and Mr. Lion has a gift to take to the tree. If you have a Christmas tree in your room, students can walk toward the tree and eventually place their gifts under it. If there is no tree, you can make one from butcher paper to hang on the wall. Students can set their gifts on the floor in front of it. You will need the following props for gifts (or you may use wrapped boxes): light brown paper scroll, a small green ball, an egg (plastic), a brush, a pillow, and a pencil.

If the classroom is small or staging area is limited, you may want to spread the readers around the room and have the children turn in their seats as Mr. and Mrs. Rabbit travel around the room to pick up the other characters. This type of staging would enhance the impression of a long walk and provide a good introduction to theatre-in-the-round. You might also choose to scatter the different readers in different rows in the classroom, then have Mr. and Mrs. Rabbit thread through the rows as they gather the other characters. This would increase the walking distance and involve all of the class. The behavior of your class should dictate which way you choose to present this script.

CHARACTERS

Narrator, Cat, Mrs. Rabbit, Mr. Rabbit, Black Hen, Pig, Goose, Cow, Mr. Giraffe, and Mr. Lion.

---

*Adapted from Phila B. Bowman, "The Christmas Tree," in *The Little Brown Bowl* (New York: Thomas Wilson and Sons, 1945).

The Christmas Tree

Narrator:

One Christmas Eve, Mr. and Mrs. Rabbit were sitting at home, alone and bored. They decided to leave their warm home and go to the place where the Christmas tree candles were shining bright. They also decided to take a gift with them to put under the tree. Their gift was a birch-bark scroll. On this scroll, all of the visitors to the Christmas tree could sign their names. Mr. and Mrs. Rabbit wore their warmest winter coats and began their journey.

Cat:

Where are you going tonight, Mr. and Mrs. Rabbit?

Mrs. Rabbit:

We go to where the Christmas tree candles are bright.

Cat:

May I go with you?

Mr. Rabbit:

If you bring a gift and walk close by my side.

Cat:

I will bring my catnip ball. It is my newest toy. It will make a fine gift for a kitten.

Narrator:

As they walked along toward the Christmas tree, they came upon a group of friends.

Black Hen:

Where are you all going, dear Cat?

Cat:

We go to where the Christmas tree candles are bright.

Pig:

May we go with you?

Cat:

If you each bring a present. You must follow close by my side.

Black Hen:

I will bring an egg, the very best egg I can lay.

Pig:

I can't bring a gift. I want them all for myself.

Mrs. Rabbit:

Oh, no! Think of having no gifts for the Christmas tree. Why, everyone gives something for Christmas. Even a pig!

Pig:

I am sorry. I was wrong. I could give a fine brush made from my bristles.

Goose:

What a nice gift! I, too, will give something of myself. I shall give a down pillow made from my best feathers. And I shall be very proud to walk close beside you, Pig. What about you, Cow? What will you bring?

Cow:

Oh, that is easy! I will bring a pail full of cream milk every morning and every night. I will give enough so that everyone shall have a drink.

Narrator:

So, with all of their gifts in hand, the animals continued their journey toward the Christmas tree candles.

Mrs. Rabbit:

Oh, look! There is the Christmas tree. Look at all of the candles burning so bright. Mr. Giraffe, what are you doing?

Mr. Giraffe:

Why, I am the one who hangs the smaller gifts on the tree.

Mr. Rabbit:

Do you want our gifts?

Mr. Giraffe:

Just a moment. Mr. Lion will be out to tell you what you must do. I will call him for you. Oh, Mr. Lion . . .

Mr. Lion:

Yes, Mr. Giraffe, what do you need?

Mr. Giraffe:

Mr. Lion, we have some more guests.

Mr. Lion:
Where are you going tonight, my children?

Mrs. Rabbit:
We go to where the Christmas tree candles are bright.

Mr. Lion:
As you can see, you have come to the tree. Did you bring gifts that we can add to the others under the tree? As you know, he who at Christmas gives not, is not blessed.

Mr. Rabbit:
We all have gifts to give.

Mr. Lion:
Then lay them under the tree. Your gifts are good, my children. For every gift made cheerfully, the Christmas tree glows more brightly. While we wait for the children, why don't you join in singing with the others?

Narrator:
And so they did. They all sang and marched around the Christmas tree together. When it was time to go, they each received a gift to take with them. They had not only found the Christmas tree with the shining candles, but they went home knowing the true meaning of Christmas.

A Kidnapped Santa Claus*

BACKGROUND INFORMATION

This story is about five mischievous spirits who do not want Santa Claus to continue to make children happy. The spirits have a goal: to entice the children of Laughing Valley into their caves, where they will encourage the children to adopt their negative character traits. But because Santa Claus provides such a positive role model, the children are happy and stay away. The spirits therefore kidnap Santa on Christmas Eve. When Santa fails to leave the children presents, the spirits hope the young people will become disenchanted and come to the caves of the mischievous spirits for friendship.

STAGING

The Narrator should stand to one side of the stage. Santa should be sitting on the opposite side of the stage, working on his toys. As the story opens, the five spirits should be sitting in a semicircle in the center of the stage. When they try to stop Santa from delivering his gifts, the spirits will move to Santa's side of the performance area. Once Santa is kidnapped, the only spirits that should remain onstage are Malice and Repentance, who will talk with Santa. These discussions with Santa should take place center stage.

CHARACTERS

Narrator, Selfishness, Envy, Hatred, Malice, Repentance, and Santa Claus.

---

*Adapted from L. Frank Baum, "A Kidnapped Santa Claus," in *A Christmas Feast*, edited by J. Charlton and Barbara Gibson (New York: Doubleday, 1976).

A Kidnapped Santa Claus

Narrator:

In the mountains of Laughing Valley, the home of Santa Claus, live five mischievous spirits—Envy, Selfishness, Hatred, Malice, and Repentance. Each has his or her own cave and hates Santa because he makes the children of Laughing Valley so happy.

To get into the caves of these spirits, one must go through a beautifully carved and decorated entrance. This leads first to the cave of Selfishness, then to the cave of Envy. From there, one enters the cave of Hatred, and then the cave of Malice, a dark, fearful cave situated in the heart of the mountain. From each of these four caves, a tunnel leads to the cave of Repentance.

As we listen in on the five mischievous spirits of the caves, we hear them plotting the fate of Santa Claus.

Selfishness:

I am really getting lonesome. Santa Claus distributes so many pretty Christmas gifts to all of the children. Through his example, they become happy and generous. And then they do not come to my cave.

Envy:

I have the same problem. The little ones seem quite content with Santa Claus. There are few, indeed, that I can coax into becoming envious.

Hatred:

And that makes it even worse for me! For if no children pass through your caves, none will come to mine.

Malice:

Nor mine!

Repentance:

As for me, it's easy to see that if children do not visit your caves, they have no need to visit mine. I am quite as neglected as you are.

Envy:

And all because of Santa Claus! He is simply ruining our business. Something must be done at once!

Selfishness:

I think we should try to visit him, one by one, and see if we can't convince him to stop making his toys and giving them to the children.

Narrator:

The other spirits agreed, and the next day they begin their visits to Santa Claus. Selfishness was the first to go to Santa's shop.

Selfishness:

Santa, good day. These toys you make are wonderfully bright and pretty. You spend so much time on them and do such a wonderful job. Why don't you keep them for yourself? It seems such a pity to give them to the boys and girls, who really don't appreciate them. Why, in no time at all, they are broken or destroyed!

Santa Claus:

Nonsense. If I can make children happy for only one day with my toys, then I am happy.

Selfishness:

(After returning to the caves) I have failed. Santa is not selfish at all. Envy, tomorrow you try to change Santa's mind.

Narrator:

The next day, Envy entered Santa's shop.

Envy:

Santa, why do you go to all of this trouble? The toy shops are full of playthings quite as pretty as these you waste your time making. What a shame these shops should interfere with your business. With their machines, they make toys so much quicker than you can. Plus, they sell them for money. You just give yours away! You get nothing for all of your hard work. Perhaps you should begin selling your toys.

Santa Claus:

Nonsense! I do not want to be rich. I want children to be happy. My work is a labor of love and kindness. Even though I work so hard all year to make toys for one special night, children also deserve the toys that they can buy in the toy shops. After all, toys get broken, and children must be amused all year, not just at Christmas.

Envy:

(Returning to the caves) I, too, have failed. Hatred, why don't you try tomorrow?

Narrator:

On the third day, Hatred went to Santa's shop to see if he could change Santa's plans.

Hatred:

Good morning, Santa. I have bad news for you.

Santa Claus:

Then run away with you, like a good fellow. Bad news is something that should be kept a secret and not shared with others.

Hatred:

You cannot escape this news. In the world there are a good many people who do not believe in Santa Claus. They have wronged you and should be bitterly hated.

Santa Claus:

Stuff and rubbish!

Hatred:

There are those who resent your making children happy. There are others who sneer at you and call you a foolish old man. You should get revenge on these people.

Santa Claus:

I don't hate them. They do me no harm. They only harm their children by making them unhappy.

Narrator:

Hatred also returned to the cave a failure. However, he had devised a plan on his way back to the caves.

Hatred:

I, too, have failed! We all know that as long as Santa is in Laughing Valley, he is protected by his ryls and knooks, the good elves that they are. But on Christmas Eve, he leaves the valley. Here is my plan. On Christmas Eve, when the sleigh is full of toys and Santa flies out of the valley, we shall throw a rope around Santa and pull him out of the sleigh. What do you say?

Narrator:

Because they knew of no other way to stop Santa Claus, they all agreed to this plan. On Christmas Eve they did exactly as Hatred had suggested. They kidnapped Santa. His elves, the ryls and knooks, were at a loss without him. But they knew the presents had to be delivered to the children. Doing the best they could, they delivered all of the gifts. But for the first time ever, the reindeer entered Laughing Valley in full daylight because it took them so long to do Santa's job. Meanwhile, in the cave, Santa was tied to a chair, unable to leave.

Malice:

The children are waking up, Santa! They are waking up to find Santa has failed them. Empty stockings. No presents. No "Ho, Ho, Ho's." Only tears and anger. Our caves will be full of children today. They will never believe in you again, Santa.

Repentance:
Let me talk to Santa alone, Malice. Go see if the children are coming yet. Santa, my brothers do not trust me very much. But it is morning now, and our mischief is done. You cannot visit the children for another year! We have accomplished our plan.

Santa Claus:
That is true. Christmas Eve is past.

Repentance:
The little ones will be greatly disappointed, but that cannot be helped. Their grief will make them envious, selfish, hateful, and malicious. They will come to our caves, and I will lead them into my cave of repentance.

Santa Claus:
Do you ever repent, yourself?

Repentance:
Oh, yes indeed! Even now I am repenting having helped in your capture. Of course, if there is no evil thought or deed, there is no repentance.

Santa Claus:
So I understand. Those who avoid evil need never visit your cave.

Repentance:
Quite true. I do hope you will forgive me, Santa. I am not all bad. I believe I accomplish a great deal in the world. Come to think of it, in order to repent completely, I will let you go. I hope you will forgive me for my part in this plan.

Santa Claus:
I bear you no malice. I am sure the world would be a dreary place without you. Merry Christmas.

Narrator:
When Santa arrived at his shop, his ryls and knooks, the good elves, were very happy to see him. They told him that all of the toys had been delivered, just as he would have done. As for the five mischievous spirits, they were filled with anger and chagrin when they realized that their clever plan had not worked. Realizing no one on Christmas Day had become envious, malicious, hateful, or selfish, they never again attempted to interfere with Santa's journey on Christmas Eve.

Christmas

The Legend of Artaban*

BACKGROUND INFORMATION

This is the story of Artaban, the fourth Wise Man who sought out the baby Jesus, King of the Jews. As the birth of Christ becomes imminent, three wise men have already left to find the baby. Artaban seeks to convince the remaining Magi that the time has come to begin their journey, but they doubt him. When they decline to accompany him on his search for the Christ Child, Artaban decides to set out on his own to find the other Magi and the Baby.

STAGING

The Narrator should stand at a lectern to one side of the performance area. The actors should enter stage left and exit stage right. Artaban will remain onstage at all times as he meets with the various other characters. As the story opens, Artaban and his friends, the well-known Three Wise Men, should be center stage in a semicircle. The friends should exit, and the dying man should enter to the far left side of the stage. The scene with the Captain and Mother should take place stage center. The scene with the Man in the Street should take place on the right, with the action moving toward center stage for the final scene. If there is not enough space for this type of movement, a temporary screen should be set up to provide a "backstage" area that performers can go to when they are not involved in the action. Audience members can add appropriate sounds during the scene with the Mother and during the street scene at the end.

CHARACTERS

Narrator, Artaban, 1st Friend, 2nd Friend, 3rd Friend, Dying Man, Mother (with baby), Captain, Man in the Street, and Jesus, King of the Jews. Optional: Man in the Street's lines could be split among up to three readers. Also, soldiers could accompany the Captain.

*Adapted from Henry Van Dyke, "The Other Wise Man," in *Book of Christmas*, edited by Pearl S. Buck (New York: Simon & Schuster, 1974).

The Legend of Artaban

Narrator:

During the reign of Caesar Augustus, when Herod was living in Jerusalem, Artaban lived in the mountains of Persia. He was a tall, dark man of about 40. He had brilliant eyes set close together under a broad brow. A sensitive man with a mission, he was a Magus, a member of an ancient priesthood. As the story opens, he and a group of friends are seated in his home discussing the prophecies of the stars. Already, three Magi have left Persia to search for the King of the Jews. Artaban encourages his friends to join him in this search.

Artaban:

The stars and numbers contain hidden meanings and prophecies that are revealed to us, the Magi. The prophecies say that this is the year the King of Israel will be born in Jerusalem. I have been waiting—along with others—for a certain star to appear in the heavens to begin my journey to find this King. In preparation, I have sold my house and all that I own. With the money, I have bought three jewels to give to the King. My friends, I believe the star has appeared and the time has come. I have asked you here tonight to invite you to go with me to find the King. It would be wonderful to take this journey together. This King is worthy of our humble service.

1st Friend:

Artaban, my friend. As much as I would like to travel with you on this journey, it is impossible. I cannot leave my family behind to chase after a star and a King whose existence is uncertain.

2nd Friend:

I agree. Also, I have a business to attend to. You surely can't expect us to just leave everything behind on the readings of stars and numbers, can you?

3rd Friend:

My son, it may be that this will be the star to show the way to the King. Yet, it could be only a shadow of that star, and we will search and find nothing. You alone are content that this is the star the prophecies foretold. Therefore, I fear you must travel alone. I am too old for this journey, but my heart shall be with you. Go in peace, Artaban.

Artaban:

It is the sign. The King is coming. If none of you will go with me, I will go to meet him alone.

Narrator:
After traveling for 10 days, Artaban reached Babylon. Seeing the body of a man lying in the road, Artaban got down from his horse. The man was poor and close to death.

Artaban:
God of truth and purity, direct me in Your holy path and the way of wisdom to know what to do for this man.

Dying Man:
Please, help me.

Artaban:
I will go the stream and get you some water. I also have some herbal remedies in my bag that will help you sleep. Lie still, and I will prepare these things for you.

Dying Man:
Who are you?

Artaban:
I am Artaban. I am going to Jerusalem in search of the newborn King of the Jews. I cannot stay any longer. I will leave you my bread and wine and medicines.

Dying Man:
I cannot offer you anything except thanks for your kindness. But I can tell you this: Our prophets have told us the King will not be born in Jerusalem, but in Bethlehem. Go there, Artaban. May God be with you.

Narrator:
Artaban continued his journey. When he found the place where the other Magi had stayed, he found a note they had left him. They had gone on across the desert looking for the King and urged Artaban to follow them. Artaban was upset at having missed his friends.

Artaban:
How can I cross the desert alone, with no food and this tired horse? I must return to Babylon. There I will sell my sapphire and buy a camel train and food for the journey. I may never find my friends. I wonder if I shall ever see the King? Because I stopped to help that poor man, I may be too late.

Narrator:

Upon returning to Babylon, Artaban used one of his precious jewels to purchase a camel and the supplies he would need to travel through the desert. As Artaban proceeded across the desert on the back of the camel, the days were hot and the nights were cold. The howls of jackals broke the silence of the night, keeping Artaban from resting soundly. The trip was a slow and difficult one, and seemed to go on forever. But finally he arrived at Bethlehem. He went from door to door, and upon finding a mother of a young child, he asked about his friends as she invited him inside. He discovered that the other Magi had found the King three days earlier. They had already presented their gifts and left.

Artaban:

Woman, tell me—have you seen three Magi? They came to Bethlehem, as I have, to find the King of the Jews.

Mother:

The three Magi were here three days ago. They left as soon as they gave Mary, the mother of the baby, their gifts. That night, Mary, her husband Joseph, and the baby fled to Egypt.

Artaban:

Are you sure that is where they went? Say, what is all that shouting?

Mother:

It is my neighbor. She told me earlier that Herod is killing all of the babies. His soldiers must be coming this way. Oh, no! They are knocking at my door!

Artaban:

Go hide in the corner where they cannot see you when I open the door. *(Opens door)* What do you want, Captain?

Captain:

My men and I are looking for newborn children. Herod has commanded that we go door to door, searching the city for babies.

Artaban:

Can't you see that I am alone in this place and you are disturbing me? I am willing to give this jewel to a prudent captain who will leave me alone in peace.

Captain:

I am sorry to have bothered you, Sir. I can assure you, you will not be bothered any further. March on, men! There is no child here.

Artaban:

God, forgive me. I have lied to save a child. And I have now given away two of the jewels meant for my gift. Shall I ever be worthy to see the face of the King?

Mother:

Because you have saved my child's life, may the Lord bless you and keep you. May the Lord make His face to shine upon you and be gracious unto you. May the Lord lift up His countenance upon you and give you peace.

Artaban:

Thank you. You will be safe now. I must resume my search.

Narrator:

Artaban continued to travel in search of the child. He traveled throughout Egypt. Everywhere he went, there were people in need. He fed the hungry, clothed the naked, and healed the sick with his medicines. Thirty-three years had passed since he left on his quest to find the King. Finally, Artaban came to Jerusalem. He was tired, worn, and ready to die himself. Yet, he did not give up hope. As he walked through the streets of Jerusalem, people passed him as they hurried to the crucifixion of the King of the Jews. He stopped a man in passing, asking . . .

Artaban:

Where are you going?

Man in the Street:

To Golgotha, outside the city walls. There is to be an execution. Haven't you heard?

Artaban:

No. I have just arrived in town. Tell me, what is going on?

Man in the Street:

Two famous robbers are to be crucified, and with them, another man they call Jesus of Nazareth. This Jesus is a man who has done many wonderful works among the people. The people love him dearly. But the priests and elders have said that he must die. He says he is the Son of God. Pilate has sent him to the cross because he said he was the King of the Jews.

Artaban:

How strange are the ways of God! At last I find the King, and he is in the hands of his enemies. I come in time to offer my last possession, a pearl. I wanted to give it to him at his birth. Now I must give it to him at his death.

Man in the Street:

Well, you'd better hurry if you want to see him at all. Follow me. I will get you there quickly.

Narrator:

Artaban followed the stranger quickly through the streets of Jerusalem to the hill of Golgotha. There Artaban saw the one he had been searching for for so many years. Artaban went to the foot of the cross.

Artaban:

This is your ransom, King of the Jews. This pearl I have carried for 33 years. It is all I have left of the jewels I wished to give you upon your birth. Instead, I present it to you at your death.

Narrator:

A great tremor ran through the earth. People and soldiers ran in fear. Artaban stood below the cross, looking up at the face of the King of the Jews. A brick flew through the air, hitting Artaban on the temple. He fell onto the ground at the feet of the King.

Jesus, King of the Jews:

I say unto thee, inasmuch as thou hast done it unto one of the least of these my brethren, thou hast done it unto me.

Narrator:

As Artaban listened to the words of the King, a calm radiance lighted his pale face. He feared nothing because he now knew he had done the best in life that he could do. One last breath escaped his lips as Artaban's journey ended. His treasures were accepted, and he had successfully completed his quest. He had found the King at last.

The Legend of the Christ Child*

BACKGROUND INFORMATION

This story is based on a legend that on Christmas Eve the Christ Child returns, roaming through towns looking for someone who will invite him in for the evening. The legend has been rewritten here so that the story is more easily readable; the original had a slightly halting language pattern that made reading it rather difficult for children. Some explanation has also been added to make the legend more understandable.

STAGING

The family should assemble center stage, with the Narrator to one side. The wandering Little Boy should approach center stage from the other side. A chair for the Mother should be placed slightly to the side of center; the Daughter and Son will gather on the floor in front of her.

CHARACTERS

Narrator, Mother, Daughter, Son, and Little Boy (the Christ Child).

*Adapted from Elizabeth Harrison, "The Legend of the Christ Child," in *Merry Christmas to You* (New York: E. P. Dutton, 1965).

The Legend of the Christ Child

Narrator:

There was once a very small child who wandered throughout a very large city, with nowhere to go on a cold and bitter Christmas Eve. As he walked down the streets of the town, he stopped at several different homes, hoping someone would let him in. He was cold and hungry. And it was Christmas Eve.

Yet, at each home he stopped at, he was turned away. Finally, as the hours passed, he became colder. The night grew later and the wind grew stronger. He had come to the end of the street, and no one had let him in. Those who had passed him on the streets had ignored him. Suddenly, a shaft of light broke through the darkness, and the child ran to the window it was streaming from.

As the child looked past the candle in the window, he saw a mother and her two children sitting in front of a warm fire. She was reading the children a story.

Mother:

And when the Child arrived at the home of someone who would let Him in, He would turn into a spirit and leave. In amazement, the family would realize the Christ Child had been in their home.

Daughter:

Is that a true story, Mother?

Mother:

I am not sure. However, I have heard people say it has happened to them. I don't know that it has, but wouldn't it be a wonderful thing if the story were true and we had a chance to see the Christ Child?

Daughter:

What was that noise, Mother?

Mother:

I think it was someone tapping on the door. Go quickly and open it, dear. It is too bitter a night for anyone to stand in the cold. Perhaps someone is seeking shelter from the storm.

Daughter:

Oh, Mother, I think it was just the bough of the tree tapping against the windowpane. Do please read another story.

Mother:
Oh, no, my daughter. Listen. I hear the tapping again. Run quickly and open the door. We shouldn't let anyone stay out on such a cold Christmas Eve.

Son:
I'll go, Mother.

Narrator:
As the son opened the door, he found standing there a child, no bigger than himself.

Daughter:
Mother, it is a little boy.

Mother:
Oh, you poor, poor child. Come in and warm yourself. He must be very cold. We must help him get warm quickly. Daughter, go get a blanket from the bed to wrap around him. Child, come sit on my lap by the fire until you have become warm.

Daughter:
What else can I do to help, Mother?

Mother:
You can both rub his hands so they begin to warm up.

Daughter:
Are you hungry, little boy?

Little Boy:
Oh, yes! I have not eaten all day.

Mother:
Daughter, go to the kitchen and bring him a bowl of bread with warm milk.

Son:
May we light the Christmas tree and let him see how beautiful it is?

Mother:
Yes, that sounds like a wonderful idea. Are you warmer now, little boy?

Little Boy:
Yes, thank you. And thank you for the food. It was very kind of you.

Daughter:

Mother, may we share our Christmas with him? We don't have any presents for him, but maybe if we give him our love, that would be a nice Christmas gift.

Mother:

That sounds like a good idea. Child, now that you are warm, would you like to move closer to the tree?

Little Boy:

Oh, yes, thank you.

Narrator:

The family and the little boy stood around the beautiful Christmas tree. While they stood there, the little boy's appearance began to change.

Daughter:

Mother, look! His clothes! They are no longer ragged. They have become white!

Son:

Mother, look! Is that a halo around his head?

Mother:

Shh, children. Be very quiet. I do not know what is happening. Let's just watch and see.

Son:

Mother, look! He is rising in the air. Our ceiling is opening up, and he is going out!

Daughter:

Mother, is that the Christ Child?

Mother:

Yes, children. I believe it is. It has happened just as the legend was written. He does go from door to door until someone lets Him in. Only those who let Him in ever see this marvelous vision. I wonder how many homes turned Him away before He came to us?

Narrator:

This story has been passed down through the ages. Perhaps it is in all of our hearts to see the Christ Child, if we but take the time to look on Christmas Eve.

The Seven Days of Kwanzaa

BACKGROUND INFORMATION

Kwanzaa is an African-American celebration that runs for seven days, from December 26 to January 1. The celebration began in 1986 as a way to incorporate the agricultural rites of Africa into the life of the African American. Each day celebrates a different principle, symbolized by the lighting of a candle. Also, an agricultural rite is celebrated, using a particular symbol assigned to that rite. This script is unlike others in the collection in that it is more of an educational tool than a simple celebration of a holiday; it provides the whole concept behind Kwanzaa. African terms are included in parentheses. The three children in the script are not named, which allows the teacher to assign the parts without regard to the sex of the child. You may want to alter the script so the names of the children reading the parts replace the prompts "1st Child," "2nd Child," "3rd Child." Kwanzaa "cuts through religious celebrations and across social and political perspective in an attempt to blend the African culture with the Afro-American life-style," according to James C. Anyike. Anyike's *Afro-American Holidays* provides information on Kwanzaa and other celebrations.

STAGING

Because there is little need for movement in this script, the Narrator and readers can all be seated stage center on stools or chairs. The Narrator should sit off to one side. The Children and Mother should face each other in a semicircle, as if they are sitting around a kitchen table.

CHARACTERS

Narrator, Mother, 1st Child, 2nd Child, and 3rd Child.

The Seven Days of Kwanzaa

Narrator:

Kwanzaa is an African-American celebration that takes place for seven days after Christmas. It begins on December 26th and ends on January 1st. Many African Americans are still learning about this celebration, as is the family in our script today. The children have just come home from school and are having a snack as they talk with their mother about their day at school.

Mother:

How was your day at school? Anything new or exciting happen?

1st Child:

No. It was boring as always.

2nd Child:

My day wasn't boring.

Mother:

Oh, really! What was your day like?

2nd Child:

We learned about Kwanzaa today.

3rd Child:

What is Kwanzaa?

2nd Child:

It is an African-American celebration.

Mother:

Kwanzaa. I don't believe I've heard of it. What is it?

2nd Child:

It is a celebration of Africa, our ancestors, and us.

1st Child:

When is it?

2nd Child:

It begins on December 26th and ends on January 1st.

1st Child:
That's a long celebration!

Mother:
I hope you don't think you'll get presents every day of Kwanzaa.

2nd Child:
Oh, no, Mother. It isn't about getting presents. It is about ideas and principles.

3rd Child:
What is a principle?

Mother:
It is a law or idea that everyone agrees to and uses to make life better.

1st Child:
Can we celebrate Kwanzaa this year?

Mother:
Well, if I know what to do and what the principles are, I guess we can. Tell me what I need to know and what we need to get to celebrate Kwanzaa.

2nd Child:
Oh, that's easy. I have all that information on my worksheet from school. I'll go get it out of my bookbag.

Mother:
While you are doing that, why don't you two get some paper and pencils so we can make lists and plans to celebrate Kwanzaa.

Narrator:
The children hurry to get the necessary materials. Upon returning to the kitchen table, they make a list of all of the items Mother will need to buy for the celebration and to learn about the seven principles.

2nd Child:
We will need seven candles. One is black, three are red, and three are green. Then we need a candle holder for the seven candles, a straw mat, a single candle holder, fruits, vegetables, an ear of corn, a unity cup, and small wrapped gifts.

3rd Child:
Why do we need all of those things?

2nd Child:
The candles stand for the seven principles, and each item stands for a special agricultural rite.

1st Child:
I thought you said there were no presents.

2nd Child:
There aren't.

1st Child:
You said we needed wrapped gifts.

2nd Child:
Well, yes, but those represent gifts, they're not actually gifts.

1st Child:
I'm confused. First you say no presents, now you say wrapped presents. And what is an agricultural rite?

Mother:
(Speaking to the 1st Child) I am sure you are confused because this is new to all of us. *(Speaking to the 2nd Child)* Why don't you explain each day to us just as we would celebrate it.

2nd Child:
That's easy. On the first day we light the black candle in the center of the big candle holder. On one side of it are the three green candles, and on the other are the three red candles. The black candle stands for unity (*Umoja*). With the lighting of the black candle, we also put down the straw mat. The mat represents our African and American traditions and history.

3rd Child:
I don't know what you mean by traditions.

Mother:
Traditions are ways of doing things that people pass down from generation to generation. They help us remember the past. Most holidays we celebrate are full of traditions. They were begun many years ago and we just keep practicing them year after year. In this celebration we will learn about some of the traditions from our ancestors long ago in Africa.

3rd Child:
Do you know any?

Mother:
Yes, I know of a few things. I guess I'll have to talk to Grandma about them, too. That way I won't forget the most important ones in our family. What do we do on the second day?

2nd Child:
We relight the black candle and one of the colored candles. Then we add an empty single candle holder (which is called *Kinara*). This stands for the continent of Africa and our ancestors. On the third day, we will relight the two candles and one of the remaining color so that we have three candles lit, one of each color. Then we will add the fruits and vegetables, which stand for the rewards of our collective labor.

1st Child:
Won't they spoil?

Mother:
I guess real ones might. Perhaps we can buy some plastic ones and then save them for next year. What are the two principles that we light the candles for on the second and third day?

2nd Child:
On the second day it is self-determination (*Kujichagulia*), and on the fourth day it is our collective work and responsibility (*Ujima*).

3rd Child:
What do you mean by collective?

Mother:
That which we do together as a family or a group of people, like sharing the chores or helping others. No one can get along without help from others. What is the fourth day about?

2nd Child:
On the fourth day we relight the candles and light one more colored one to represent cooperative economics (*Uiamaa*), and we add the ear of corn to represent the offspring of our people.

1st Child:
Offspring? There sure are a lot of new words I don't know. This is beginning to sound like school.

Mother:

I guess it does. But I think you will understand all of this better after we celebrate each of these days. We will discuss each of these ideas as we light the candles each day. So, go ahead and tell us about the other days.

2nd Child:

On the fifth day we light five candles, and the fifth candle stands for purpose (*Nia*). We also add the communal unity cup.

3rd Child:

What is a unity cup?

2nd Child:

It is a single cup that everyone drinks out of rather than each person having his or her own. People use it to show they all agree on something. On the sixth day, after we relight the five candles, we light a sixth candle, which stands for creativity (*Kuumba*), and we will add the wrapped gifts.

1st Child:

What will be in the boxes?

2nd Child:

I told you before, they aren't gifts for us; they represent gifts. They remind us that we must work hard to deserve rewards or to achieve something. Kwanzaa isn't like Christmas, when you get presents. These gifts are supposed to make you think about your year. They make you appreciate all of the rewards you have already gotten and consider how well you have done during the year. The last day, all seven candles are lit (this is known as *Ngugo Saba*), and we consider the last principle, faith (*Imani*). That is how the seven days of Kwanzaa are celebrated.

Mother:

It sounds wonderful. I'll get everything we need between now and then so we can celebrate every day. In fact, why don't we ask your grandmother to come for each celebration so she can help us learn about our past?

3rd Child:

Can we invite friends, too?

Mother:

I guess so. That would be a good way to learn about our past and ourselves. That's a good idea. Right now, however, I need the three of you to clear off the table and go do your homework while I fix dinner.